Awakening to God provides some wonde[...]
follower to be empowered, envisioned, and equipped to [...]
family and friends with the wonderful news of Jesus Christ.
Following Jesus' instructions, Gerard Long shows that evangelism
should start and continue with God's love and power being
poured into our hearts by the Holy Spirit. He points out that
the first 120 Christ followers turned the world upside down, and
there is still great hope for America to have another awakening!

MARK BATTERSON
New York Times bestselling author of *The Circle Maker* and lead pastor
of National Community Church in Washington, DC

My life's mission is to be a loving teacher and example of simple
truths, helping myself and others to awaken to the presence of
God in our lives. That was not my life's mission until my early
fifties, when my wonderful Christian friends awakened me
to the presence of God in my life. Read Gerard Long's book,
Awakening to God, so you can become more awake yourself and
become that kind of friend to others.

KEN BLANCHARD
coauthor of *The One Minute Manager* and *Lead Like Jesus*

Awakening to God is truly a wake-up call for us all to be on
mission, wherever we are living life, and to discover the ultimate
and true plan God has for each of us. Gerard's experience in
the corporate world, along with his years of leadership with
Alpha, gives him major street cred to write this book. I highly
recommend it!

BRAD LOMENICK
author of *The Catalyst Leader*, former president and key visionary of
Catalyst

Gerard Long has experienced hard battles in life, but his faith in Jesus Christ stands undiminished. It is inspiring that his desire to share his faith is stronger than ever.

NICKY GUMBEL
pioneer of Alpha and senior pastor of HTB London

An inspiring book for anyone exploring the adventure of faith!

BEAR GRYLLS
adventurer, author, TV presenter

Awakening to God is a great read for anyone interested in knowing God and joining with him in his rescue mission for men and women across the globe.

ROMA DOWNEY
actor, author, producer of the major motion picture *Son of God*

Awakening to God is a must-read for pastors and church leaders. It will not only awaken you to God's call and power in your own life, but it will also help your church awaken to its full purpose and potential.

SCOTT EVANS
president of Outreach Inc.

What a story! What reality! What relief and joy and peace to be reminded of the never-ending love of God, even in the midst of excruciating pain—pain that Gerard Long and his family know all too well. In this wonderful book, Gerard shares the power and importance of spiritual awakening—that moment when a person comes alive to God through faith in his Son,

Jesus Christ. Whether you are already a follower of Jesus or still searching for spiritual reality, *Awakening to God* will arouse you out of your spiritual slumber and get you going on a life of spiritual relevance that will have eternal consequences.

LUIS PALAU
world evangelist

Gerard Long personifies the hope embedded in a classic psalm: "Sorrow may last for a night, but joy comes in the morning." His personal tragedies expose in him a faith that enables him to both move mountains and to "be still" and know that Christ is God. In his new book, *Awakening to God*, Gerard shines the light of Jesus and empowers the reader to engage in a journey of faith, love, truth, and life.

SAMUEL RODRIGUEZ
president of NHCLC, the Hispanic Evangelical Association

With gentleness, grace, and a sense of urgency, Gerard Long calls us to a great awakening that will affect us personally and in community. He focuses on our coming alive to God's love and purpose; to the Holy Spirit; to God's calling to go and make disciples; to brokenness; to eternity; and to the opportunity God gives us, and the provision he provides, to seize that opportunity. He invites us to invite others to "come and see." This is not a dry how-to book on evangelism and discipleship. Instead, it's simply one changed person sharing with the rest of us what God has done in his life and what God has in mind for ours.

DENNY RYDBERG
president of Young Life

Awakening to God is a breath of fresh air, a rejuvenating invitation to the fundamentals of Christian life and witness. If your spiritual life is in a rut and you're longing to get back to your first love, this book is for you. If you're wondering whether God has a deeper purpose for your life, this book is for you. If you've ever found yourself unsure of how to share the gospel in a world that questions the gospel's continued relevance, this book is for you.

JIM LISKE
president and CEO of Prison Fellowship Ministries

Gerard Long is a sincere, passionate man with street credibility in both the business domain and the church. In *Awakening to God*, I appreciate Gerard's straightforward way of sharing about his brokenness and the beauty of Christ in the midst of his journey. This is a practical guide for those who want to share about their relationship with Jesus in a way that is more real, supernatural, organic, and clear.

DAVE GIBBONS
founder of Newsong Church and XEALOTS

Gerard Long has written a vital and vibrant book that will both encourage and challenge you. He is a man of deep experience who knows of what he speaks. Definitely a worthy read.

GREGORY W. SLAYTON
author of the national bestseller *Be a Better Dad Today: Ten Tools Every Father Needs*

Awakening to God shows us how God's love can enter any situation and bring true transformation. From the lessons of a life filled with joys and sorrows, Long beautifully shows how God loves us, equips us, and sustains us as we go and make disciples.

KERRY KNOTT
president of the C. S. Lewis Institute

The early church grew exponentially because people were drawn by their passion for Jesus. Today, we have the same opportunity—and the same responsibility. *Awakening to God* will renew your spirit and inspire you to be more intentional about building relationships with people who don't know God.

MAC MCQUISTON
CEO/president of the CEO Forum, Inc.

Awakening to God not only tells the surprising, moving story of how God changed one man's life forever, it is a practical, gentle wake-up call to sleeping people everywhere. If you're stuck in a rut, underwhelmed by life, and not sure your life could ever be much different, this is the book for you!

DON EVERTS
author of *Go and Do: Becoming a Missional Christian*

AWAKENING TO GOD

Discovering his power and your purpose

GERARD LONG

TYNDALE™
MOMENTUM

An Imprint of
Tyndale House Publishers, Inc.

Visit Tyndale online at www.tyndale.com.

Visit Tyndale Momentum online at www.tyndalemomentum.com.

TYNDALE is a registered trademark of Tyndale House Publishers, Inc. *Tyndale Momentum* and the Tyndale Momentum logo are trademarks of Tyndale House Publishers, Inc. Tyndale Momentum is an imprint of Tyndale House Publishers, Inc.

Awakening to God: Discovering His Power and Your Purpose

Copyright © 2014 by Gerard B. Long. All rights reserved.

Designed by Mark Anthony Lane II

Published in association with the literary agency of Wolgemuth and Associates, Inc., 8600 Crestgate Circle, Orlando, FL 32819.

Library of Congress Cataloging-in-Publication Data

Long, Gerard
  Awakening to God : discovering his power and your purpose / Gerard Long.
    pages cm
  Includes bibliographical references.
  ISBN 978-1-4143-9628-6 (sc)
  1. Religious awakening—Christianity. I. Title.
  BV4509.5.L65 2014
  269—dc23   2014019827

Printed in the United States of America

20	19	18	17	16	15	14
7	6	5	4	3	2	1

To my darling Jeannie, whom I love with all my heart. You are my soul mate, my best friend, my prayer partner, and my wife. Thank you for journeying with me over the mountains and through the valleys until we arrive safely home!

Contents

Foreword

LET ME BEGIN by saying I love Alpha, the outreach organization whose US division Gerard Long has led since 2006. At Willow Creek, Alpha is the primary tool we use to help people discover satisfying answers to their questions about faith, God, and Christianity. And we are not alone. Through the Alpha course, millions of people around the world have awakened to God, understood for the first time the basics of following Christ, and found meaning and purpose for their lives.

The work Gerard and others are doing through Alpha is the most important in the world. In this book, Gerard invites you on a journey of awakening to what matters most in this life. Through the story of his own series of awakenings—some of them resulting from great personal tragedy— he challenges you to embrace the awakenings God desires for each of us:

- Awakening to his love, purpose, and power for living
- Awakening to the brokenness of life on this earth and the promise of a different life in the next reality
- Awakening to our ultimate callings
- Awakening to his strategy for making disciples.

The pages of this book hold the capacity to stir a Spirit-prodded appetite for God's awakenings in your life as a Christ follower. As you read, may you invite God to awaken in you a greater awareness of his presence and activity in your life—and in the lives of those you impact in his name.

Bill Hybels

Introduction

How beautiful on the mountains are the feet of those
who bring good news, who proclaim peace, who
bring good tidings, who proclaim salvation.

ISAIAH 52:7

IN MY WORK for Alpha, a not-for-profit ministry that invites people to learn the basics of Christianity in a relaxed, welcoming, and engaging atmosphere, I travel extensively throughout the United States. People I meet who are aware of my background in finance will often ask me why and how I left the corporate world to work for a nonprofit organization—and especially to work for Alpha, whose low-key, informal approach to evangelism seems incompatible with their image of a buttoned-down banker.

Over time, I've come to realize that the answer to their question involves one of several awakenings I've had—times when God has either roused me from a spiritual slumber or has otherwise redirected my steps to be more in line with his purpose for my life. Further, I've found that these awakenings are "common to mankind"—that is, they're awakenings that God desires for every person to have; in fact, they're essential to God's work in our lives and in our world.

I've noticed over the past few years that many Christians

I meet feel beaten down in their faith. They are disappointed and frustrated by the lack of power and impact they've had for the Kingdom of God. They've been followers of Christ for years, and yet they feel as if they haven't effectively lived out the Great Commission to make disciples of all nations. Instead, they're stuck with a mixture of fear and concern that they don't know enough to be able to share their faith with others.

Many of these Christians are passionate about their faith, but they're looking for practical guidance that will enable them to share God's love with their family, friends, neighbors, and coworkers. Does that sound familiar?

I have no doubt that you, too, are concerned for the souls of the people around you, and yet the thought of another "evangelism program" can seem daunting—even a plan designed by Jesus himself. But every evangelistic effort at its core is simply an invitation to "come and see."[1] We have utilized this simple model to great effect within the Alpha Course, and I'd like to show you how to apply it even more generally in your life.

Jesus told his disciples to "go into all the world," and he promised he would make them "fishers of men."[2] They promptly went out and turned the world upside down. That same promise and prospect is available to us today.

My aim in these pages is to give you hope that a fresh experience of God is possible, and to inspire you to "go and tell" your friends and neighbors, so that they will "come and see" and be captivated by the good news of God's love and his

Kingdom. Yet, even as I seek to present my case with gentleness and grace, I can only hope to adequately convey the urgency of God's calling: "*Wake up!* Strengthen what remains and is about to die, for I have found your deeds unfinished."[3]

It's time for a fresh awakening of our hearts to God. Let's go turn the world upside down again.

1

AWAKENING TO GOD'S LOVE AND PURPOSE

"For I know the plans I have for you," declares the LORD, "plans to prosper you and not to harm you, plans to give you hope and a future."
JEREMIAH 29:11

I STILL REMEMBER the day my eyes were opened—Valentine's Day 1980. I was in my dormitory room at Loughborough University, in England, and had received a letter from my brother Will the day before. He wrote about many things, but one line in particular fairly leapt off the page at me: *God has got a plan for your life made out of perfect love.*

Until that day, I had been going my own way for several years. Though raised by Christian parents in a loving home, I had, like many young people, decided to walk away from the church. I had been a Christian since I was five or six years old, but I seemed to have little desire to truly live for Jesus—that is, to conform my will and my ways to his. I was frustrated and disappointed with myself, and more than a little embarrassed about my faith. I can remember dreading the thought of having my friends come by for tea, because my mum would say grace beforehand and I was afraid of what my friends would think. And I recall riding to church on Sundays, desperately hoping I wouldn't be spotted by anyone I knew.

I knew I was a hypocrite, *saying* one thing but *living* something else entirely, but I had reached a point where I really didn't care. My head was in it, but my heart was far removed. When I was sixteen, I decided to stop trying to be a good Christian. I'd had enough of the dual lifestyle. I was done. The last thing I wanted to do was discourage my friends from following Jesus just because I couldn't do it.

Though I did my fair share of wayward living over the next several years—hurting many people in the process and damaging myself, as well—my real motivation was to throw myself into middle-distance running, and track soon became a replacement god for me. I ate it, slept it, and drank it—and it consumed me. I loved the adrenaline rush before a race, the simplicity and pureness of pitching my utmost against my fellow competitors over a set distance, and, of course, the triumph of breaking the tape as the front-runner.

The focus and discipline needed to accomplish my goal—to train day in and day out, whether I felt strong or weak, and whatever the weather—appealed to my character. I was proud, and my ego was boosted as I won championships and achieved recognition.[1] I reached a high level of success on the track and was elected captain of my college team, which included double Olympic champion and world-record holder Sebastian Coe. Aside from running and studying, I had little time or attention for anything else.

By my final year of college, I had a game plan of total dedication to pass my exams and to be selected to run in the Olympic Trials for Great Britain. I moved off-campus to get away from the partying, and I doubled down on my studies and training. Things started well, but then disaster struck as I incurred a serious Achilles injury, which interrupted my training for several months. Although I managed to regain some fitness to run for my college team, it wasn't enough to qualify me to compete in the Trials.

Around this same time, my future wife, Jeannie, whom I had met a couple of years earlier, went back overseas to pursue her ballet career. We had kept in touch while she was dancing with a corps de ballet in Austria, and when she'd returned to the UK, she had begun talking about our getting married. But that was definitely not a part of my egocentric plan at the time, and in my selfishness, I turned her away. Now she was back on the Continent with her troupe, and in her absence, God finally had me in a place where I could hear his voice.

On the morning of February 14, I sat alone at my desk—no music, no friends, no noise, no distractions. Just me and God. And I couldn't get Will's words out of my mind.

As I contemplated God's perfect love for me, and the thought that he had a purpose for me that I had pushed to the margins of my life, I felt the truth awaken my heart in a way I had never before experienced. Believing, as I did, that God created the universe and everything in it, it struck home with astonishing clarity that his plan for my life had to be wiser and more purposeful than my own self-absorbed ideas. This seems quite obvious in retrospect, but at the time it was a revelation.

I sat and reflected on this reality for a long time. Eventually, it seemed the only smart decision was to fully surrender my life to God. As I was drawn to prayer, I sensed the Lord saying that if he had the proper place in my life—namely, *his* will ahead of *my* will—I might not get everything I had planned on the outside, but inside I would have abundance—a life full of love, joy, peace, contentment, and purpose.

For the first time in my life, I truly understood what this meant: God created me for an intimate relationship with him. Apart from him, I am incomplete. I had been trying to fill this God-shaped void with many other things, but only he can complete me.

Scripture verses I had long since memorized and forgotten suddenly came alive for me in a new way. "For what shall it profit a man, if he shall gain the whole world, and lose his own soul?"[2] These words, which for me had been purely theoretical up to this point, now seemed as if they'd been penned just for me. What would I gain if I got everything I ever wanted— every experience and every achievement—but inside I was empty and dissatisfied? Where was the value in that?

I finally recognized that God could give me contentment

on the inside, even if I had nothing on the outside. In him alone I would have everything my soul could ever need.

When I was younger, I'd heard an analogy of salvation that compared inviting Christ into my heart to inviting him into my house. I realized that, in my earlier conversion, I had asked Jesus in the front door but had left him standing in the hallway. I hadn't wanted him to come into the other rooms— into my relationships, my work and career, my money, my future—because I wanted to control those aspects of my life. I had been a fool, thinking I knew better than the Creator of the universe what was best for my life! I had received Jesus as my Savior but not as my Lord. But now I was saying, "Jesus, I trust you and give you full permission to be Lord over every area of my life, and I believe that you know better than I do what is best for me. I not only belong to you, but I fully surrender my life to you."

As I made this decision in my mind and spoke it out loud to the empty room, it was as if God showed up in my apartment. As best I can describe it, it felt as if liquid love were being poured into my heart. It was just me and God, and his Spirit filled my life. I started to weep as I felt his loving embrace. I'd been living on my own, but now I felt as if I'd come home. I hadn't cried in seven or eight years, but I wept from the bottom of my heart as God's love filled me.

At the time, I didn't know what was going on, but now I know from Scripture that the Holy Spirit was filling my heart with love.[3] I suddenly understood the purpose for my life—to love and serve God. To no longer live for myself, but instead to live for *him*. The tears of love now turned into tears of utter joy as, for the first time in my life, I felt totally complete. None of the things on which I had previously hung my hat mattered to me as much anymore—athletics (which until then had consumed me), my relationship with Jeannie (which had been so beautiful), making money (through a successful small business I had founded on campus), and even my future. All these things I now felt free to leave in God's hands. If he wanted me to have them back to use for his service, fine; but if not, it didn't matter—I was utterly fulfilled in him.

That's not to say that every day since has been a spiritual high. But I can honestly say this was more than just a momentary, spiritual epiphany. It was a turning point, a true awakening that set my life on a different course. Instead of being self-centered, I became God-centered.

I've included this brief overview of my growing-up years because, as I've spoken to groups and individuals, I've found that people tend to relate to one part of my experience or another—whether it's walking away from God for a time, giving in to temptation and making sinful choices, going all-in on something that seems worthwhile but comes at the expense of an intimate relationship with God, or simply coming to a place where it seems there must be something more to the Christian life. Whatever it is in your life that has prompted you to pick up a book called *Awakening to God*, let me encourage you with this: *God truly does have a plan for your life made out of perfect love.* That doesn't mean your life will be perfect. But God's love for you is perfect, and when you surrender to it and allow it to permeate every part of your being—to enter every room in your house—God will fill you to overflowing with the power of his Holy Spirit.

This is the first awakening we all need—awakening to God's calling us by name, firstly to himself, but also to a perfect design for our lives made out of unconditional love.

AWAKENING TO GOD'S LORDSHIP

You will seek me and find me when you seek me with all your heart.
JEREMIAH 29:13

I encourage you to consider, and even wrestle with, the following thoughts and questions. Either God is King and Lord of your life, or someone else is—probably *you*. God created you for a relationship with him, and because he desperately loves you, he wants the very best for you: to bless you, fulfill you, and give you fullness of life, including love, joy, and peace. Also, he has given you a unique opportunity to participate with him in sharing his love with others. He has prepared, from the beginning of time, a unique plan for your life. Think of a parent who wants the best for his or her children. Despite having limited knowledge and power, the parent still knows more than the children do about what will bless them and what will harm them. Now consider that God has perfect knowledge and complete power. If you let him, he will guide you into a full and satisfying life.

Jesus showed us how to walk through life. On many

occasions, he made it clear that he was not living for his own will, but rather for God's will, to please him.[4] In doing this, he not only lived a fulfilled and complete life, but he also accomplished the eternal purpose of God, bringing forgiveness, reconciliation, and salvation to the world.

However good you may think your plan is for your life, God's plan is a lot better. His plan will give you the best possible life you can imagine. You will experience true contentment, love, joy, and peace—and God will use you to bless many other people. You will also store up for yourself "treasures in heaven"—eternal rewards.[5]

God's life will flow from within you, and it will not depend on what you have on the outside. The ways of God's Kingdom are different from the values of this world, which feed and motivate selfish desires. (What is it that causes so much trouble in the world? Is it not from people pursuing their selfish desires?) God's desire is that your inner *self* would be crucified with Christ, such that you no longer live for what *you* want but for what *he* wants.[6] If you abide in Jesus, his life flows within you.

Do you believe and trust in God enough to surrender every area of your life to him? Are you willing to say to him, "Your will be done in my relationships, my family, my possessions, my health, my career—in every choice I make"?

AWAKENING TO GOD'S LOVE

I pray that you, being rooted and established in love, may have power,
together with all the Lord's holy people, to grasp how wide and long

and high and deep is the love of Christ, and to know this love that
surpasses knowledge—that you may be filled to the measure of all the
fullness of God.

EPHESIANS 3:17-19

Four things immediately changed in my life on the day I fully
surrendered my life to Christ. First, I found I was head over
heels in love with Jesus Christ. When you really love someone, you take great pleasure in pleasing that person. This was
now all I wanted to do—to please God by doing his will.[7]

The second thing I noticed was that I had a love for God's
Word. Now that my eyes were opened, God's truth was excit-
ing and fresh to me. I found I could hardly put down my
Bible and would read it into the early hours of the morning, making copious notes. As I encountered Scriptures that
spoke to me, I began sharing them with family and friends
who were also following Christ. I realize now that my parents
were very patient during this time, as I often thought I had
come across some great revelation that no one had ever seen
before.

The third change was that I stopped swearing. Without
my even trying or thinking about it, this nasty habit just
slipped away. Also, because of my deep and passionate love
for Jesus Christ, I wanted to rid my life of anything that
would disappoint or grieve him. This desire to dedicate and
separate my life to please God (i.e., to live a holy life) flowed
out of a love from my heart, not from my head.

Finally, I developed a deep love and concern for other

people, including their current needs and their eternal destiny. In particular, I was desperate to tell them about Jesus Christ. Though the other changes were certainly remarkable, I believe this one was the most notable, in light of my past. It was as if I had discovered a gold mine with enough of the precious metal for everyone in the world. How could I keep it to myself? I had to share my discovery with other people. In particular, I wanted my friends to meet Jesus and experience the abundance of life I was now enjoying.

I remember being quite nervous as I approached the first friend with whom I planned to share the gospel. I prayed that God would help me and would open my friend's eyes to see Jesus. And then I simply stepped out, trusting God to guide me.

"Hey, Jim, I had an amazing experience the other day that has completely changed my life . . ."

I explained to him about my brother's letter and how I had reasoned that God's plan for my life had to be better than my own. I shared how I had sensed God speaking to me and how I had experienced what felt like liquid love flowing through me as I told God that I now wanted to live for him and not for myself. I don't think Jim knew quite what to say, but he didn't mock me (at least, not to my face). He simply heard me out.

With this first effort under my belt, I felt emboldened to speak to others, as well. Starting with one or two friends at a time, often over a meal or at tea, I began telling everyone I knew about my encounter with God and the new direction for my life. I was completely captivated by God's love and simply *had* to share it.

Incredibly, I found that the more I shared my faith, the more joy seemed to course through me and the more I felt God's presence within me. My friends could see that something profound had happened to me, and their mouths may have dropped open in surprise. After all, the captain of the top college track team in the country and one of the "lads" around campus was now openly following Jesus Christ.

Later that year, an evangelist named Eric Delve led a crusade on our campus. He agreed to let me share my testimony, and I invited everybody I could to come along to the meeting. My parents and my brother Will drove up for the event. The place was packed, and as the time came for me to share my story, I was literally shaking with nerves. When I was called up to speak, I attempted to take the quickest route to the microphone by leaping onto the stage. However, I miscalculated my jump, tripped, and fell flat on my face, to a roar of applause and laughter from my friends. It was all in good humor, but as I picked myself up, I discovered that the nerves had been knocked completely out of me. I found I could think clearly, and I believe the testimony I gave was relatively lucid. Ever since then, God has enabled me, even with some nerves, to speak in public.

In the thirty-four years since my heart was awakened to God's love and his purpose for my life, my love for him, for his Word, and for people has grown deeper and deeper. That is not to say that life has been easy. On the contrary, as I'll share later, I have experienced tremendous pain and suffering. But I've discovered that God is my source of love, joy, peace, strength, and wisdom. In fact, he supplies everything I need for whatever I come across on my journey. His grace really is sufficient![8]

I've learned a wonderful secret for life: how to strengthen my soul in God.[9] This flows out of simply spending time in God's presence—first on my own but also with other Christians. I've discovered that God's Word nourishes my soul and lights my path.[10] I've experienced how the Holy Spirit strengthens, empowers, and equips me for every situation. Like anyone else, I often mess up, but I've learned to quickly repent so that I don't grieve God by being out of sync with him for very long. My prayer is that you, too, will awaken to God's love and purpose for your life.

2

AWAKENING TO THE HOLY SPIRIT: POWER FOR LIVING

But you shall receive power (ability, efficiency, and might)
when the Holy Spirit has come upon you, and you shall
be My witnesses in Jerusalem and all Judea and Samaria
and to the ends (the very bounds) of the earth.

ACTS 1:8, AMP

JUST BEFORE HIS ascension to heaven, Jesus told his disciples
not to leave Jerusalem until they were filled with the Holy
Spirit.[1] On another occasion, he also said it was better that he
go away so that the disciples could receive the Holy Spirit.[2]
What do these words from Jesus tell us about the Holy Spirit?
For one thing, being filled with the Holy Spirit is essential to
being a disciple of Jesus Christ.

But what does it mean to be filled with the Holy Spirit?
In this chapter, we're going to explore the answer to that
question. I encourage you to take time to consider what Jesus
said to his disciples and to be hungry for God to speak to

your heart about the Holy Spirit's place in your life. Let me start by telling you about my own spiritual journey and my awakening to the Holy Spirit.

I'm very grateful for my family heritage. I can trace my ancestry back to the Huguenots, a group of French Calvinists who fled religious persecution in the sixteenth and seventeenth centuries. Growing up, I was impressed by my parents' walk with the Lord because it was reflected in their love for each other. Our home environment was one of acceptance and deep gratitude to God for his loving-kindness toward us. Scripture memorization was a part of my life, and I can clearly remember, at an early age, kneeling with my sister, Jax, and asking Jesus to forgive my sins, come into my heart, and be my Good Shepherd. Though I was very young, I believe this was a genuine conversion and that Christ became my Savior at that time, through the work of the Holy Spirit.

During my early childhood, my parents were part of the Exclusive Brethren, a Protestant denomination that lived up to its name by isolating its members from other followers of Jesus. By the early 1960s, my parents had left the Exclusive Brethren because of the group's excessive legalism. Though they didn't know any other Christians locally, God took care of them, and they were deeply affected by an outpouring of the Holy Spirit in the 1960s and 1970s (sometimes referred to as the Charismatic Renewal). Despite the spiritual energy of those days, balanced teaching on the person and place of the Holy Spirit seemed lacking, certainly for me as a young believer.

LIKE A DISCIPLE BEFORE PENTECOST

As I look back on the first seventeen years of my spiritual journey, and knowing what I know today, I realize I was like a disciple before Pentecost. Though I believed in Jesus, I had no power to be a witness for him. I didn't want people to know I was a Christian. I had little or no motivation to lay down my life for Christ. Yes, he was my Savior, but he wasn't my Lord. Like every Christian, I had received the Holy Spirit at salvation, but I wasn't *filled* with the Holy Spirit.[3] Though the Spirit had come in through the front door, I hadn't invited him into (or given him control over) the rest of the house. Instead, I was forfeiting the fullness of life that comes through the Holy Spirit for a counterfeit—life through the flesh.[4]

Think about the significance of Jesus' command to his disciples not to leave Jerusalem until they had been baptized with the Holy Spirit. Even though his followers had been with him constantly for three years and had witnessed the miracle of his resurrection from the dead (and even though Jesus had opened the Scriptures to them and had told them what he wanted them to do), they were *powerless* to carry out his instructions without being filled by the Holy Spirit.

I believe the same is true for us today. We desperately need to be filled with the Holy Spirit on an ongoing basis; and unless we are, we're powerless. As Billy Graham has said, "I am convinced that to be filled with the Spirit is not an option, but a necessity."[5]

Coming to this understanding gave me insight into what had happened during my early life as a follower of Jesus. Perhaps you, too, will find that this resonates with your faith walk.

When, as a young boy, I asked Jesus to forgive my sins and come into my life, I received the Holy Spirit, but I had no idea how to have an intimate relationship with him.[6] For a long time, I didn't know that it was the Holy Spirit who pours God's love into our hearts, who reveals Jesus to us. No one explained to me that the Holy Spirit is present to guide, help, encourage, and comfort us through life.[7] I didn't realize that we could resist, grieve, and quench the Holy Spirit.[8] I didn't know that we can and should keep asking God to fill us continually (again and again) with the Holy Spirit.

Years later, when I fully surrendered my life to Christ, in his mercy he filled me with his Spirit. After this happened, I was taught from Scripture that God wants to pour out his Spirit on *every* Christ follower.[9] But he's waiting for us to ask him.[10]

What about you? What have you been taught about the Holy Spirit? How well do you know who he is, what he does, and how to be filled with his power on an ongoing basis?

When I surrendered everything to God, his love filled my life. Where did this love come from? Scripture tells us: God's love is poured into our hearts by the Holy Spirit.[11] With God's love, I received power and motivation to lay down my life to be a witness for Jesus Christ.[12] As the Scripture says, "You will receive power when the Holy Spirit has come upon you, and you will be my witnesses."[13]

WHY DO WE NEED TO BE REFILLED?

I want to be clear: I'm not talking about a *second blessing*, as some would have it, but rather the *ongoing* filling of the Holy Spirit that begins at salvation. We read in the book of Acts that the disciples were filled with the Holy Spirit at Pentecost, but then we also see that they were filled again on other occasions.[14] In Paul's letter to the saints in Ephesus, he says, "Be [continually] filled with the Holy Spirit."[15] But why do we need to be filled again and again with the Holy Spirit? I believe D. L. Moody explained it well when he said, "Because I leak!"

Let me ask you a question: Was there ever a time in your Christian walk when you loved Jesus more than you do today? Was there ever a time when you had more joy and peace? Consider this: God's love toward you has never changed, and his joy and peace have been available to you, constantly, in full measure. So what happened on your end? Perhaps, like D. L. Moody, you leak!

From my own faith battle, I've seen that there are many ways to "spring a leak" and begin to lose your sense of the Holy Spirit's filling in your life. Perhaps a relationship didn't work out as you had hoped, or one or more people have hurt you deeply. (This is even more painful if those people are Christians.) Maybe you've suffered a terrible loss— bereavement, business failure, financial downturn, health concerns. Or maybe wrong teaching has drawn you away from a simple and pure devotion to Christ.[16] Sometimes it's just busyness and the pressures of life that squeeze Jesus out and keep him from being our "first love"—the one we serve and want to honor with our lives.[17]

How do these things affect our walk with Christ? They can undermine our trust in him and cause us to doubt his faithfulness and provision. We wonder, *How could God allow this to happen to me if he loves me so much?* As our hearts grow cold toward God, this affects our love for him and makes us more vulnerable to sin and unbelief.

When we stop walking in God's path and start walking in sin, we grieve the Holy Spirit.[18] When we allow unbelief to take root in our hearts, we quench the Holy Spirit.[19] When our hearts grow hard toward God, we resist the Holy Spirit.[20] He never completely leaves us, but we can begin to feel emotionally distant from him. This is a serious problem, because it's our intimacy with the Holy Spirit that gives us and others the sense of God's presence with us.

We are called to fellowship with the Holy Spirit, and we must faithfully tend our own hearts to make sure nothing spoils this relationship.[21] Thankfully, God's grace enables us to do this.

The apostle Paul told his prodigy Timothy to "fight the good fight of faith and take hold of the eternal life to which you were called when you made your confession of faith."[22] At the end of his life, Paul said, "I have fought the good fight, I have finished the race, I have kept the faith."[23] We need to keep on being filled with the Holy Spirit so that we can be continually renewed in the love of God and receive his power and grace.[24] Billy Graham summarized the process well in saying, "The filling of the Holy Spirit should not be a once-for-all event, but a continuous reality every day of our lives."[25]

Knowing the Holy Spirit gives me great hope for other people and motivates my work. So often, we try to clean up our lives by our own strength. It's clear to me—from Scripture and from my own experience—that this is impossible and only leads to failure and disappointment. Eventually, people give up and decide that God either isn't real or that he doesn't love us or care about us. This couldn't be further from the truth.

When we are in fellowship with the Holy Spirit, he produces his fruit and reveals his gifts through our lives.[26] He is the one who gives us the words to speak when our faith is challenged.[27] He is the one who convicts us when we're thinking, speaking, or doing something that hurts God.[28]

It is the Holy Spirit who gradually changes us to be more like Jesus, giving us the motivation to lay down our lives in order to do God's will.[29] I have found that the more I surrender my will to the Holy Spirit, the more Jesus is revealed *to* me and *through* me to others, and the more God seems to reign in my life. As I continue to live in the power of the Holy Spirit, being filled on a daily basis, I find I have more love, joy, peace, patience, kindness, goodness, faithfulness, gentleness, and self-control.[30] It's not *my* doing; it's what the Spirit does through me. I simply aim to keep my heart aligned with God's will.

Because of my experience of walking away from God in my youth, it's particularly tragic to me to see that close to 80 percent of young people in America today are leaving the church around the age of fifteen. The same lack of understanding I had as a teenager about the ongoing filling of the Holy Spirit seems to be symptomatic of the young people who are leaving the church in droves today.

THE ONGOING FILLING OF THE HOLY SPIRIT

Because I know firsthand that being filled with the Holy Spirit is essential, the first thing I do most mornings when I get out of bed is ask God to fill me again. I stretch my hands above my head in a gesture of surrender, to receive and acknowledge that I'm not my own, asking God to fill every part of my life. (This posture also helps to stretch out my troublesome back!) Often, but not always, I will physically experience a stirring within, manifested in great joy flowing from deep inside (regardless of whatever challenge I might be facing in my life at that time). Sometimes the presence of God is so powerful that I weep as his love washes over me. Out of these times in God's presence, and through the filling of the Holy Spirit, I find I have the grace to face whatever the day might bring. God's grace and mercy give me renewed power, passion, strength, wisdom, and whatever else I need to live abundantly that day.[31]

More than thirty-four years have gone by since my encounter with God on February 14, 1980. Compared with the seventeen previous years when I didn't know or understand the work of the Holy Spirit, the difference is like night and day. Those early years were powerless, frustrating, awkward, hypocritical, and disappointing. But ever since the Holy Spirit filled—and continually refills—my heart, I've had abundance of life, victory, triumph, blessing, and the wonderful privilege of being part of what God is doing in our day. And that is all true even though, as I'll share later on, I have been tried and tested in the valley of the shadow of death.

HOW TO BE CONTINUALLY FILLED WITH THE HOLY SPIRIT

So now, I want to challenge you: Ask God to fill you with his Holy Spirit.[32]

Wherever you are on your journey, I encourage you to make this request a regular pattern in your life, asking God daily to fill you afresh with his Holy Spirit. But before you do this, you must prepare your heart on two important points: *desire* and *trust*.

To assess your desire, ask yourself these questions: *Am I hungry for more of God in my life? Do I really want to know him more? If not, why?* This is just between you and God, so you can be completely honest. But if you believe God is good and wise and powerful, why wouldn't you want more of him in your life?

Well, you might say, *I'm not sure I want to change. I like my life as it is.*

This was exactly the reasoning I used as a teenager, when I had hold of the steering wheel of my life. But as I discovered, when you analyze that statement, it doesn't make any sense. It's illogical. How can our plans for life ever be better than God's plan? It comes down to belief and trust. That's why Jesus was always telling his disciples to *believe*,[33] not to succumb to fear but to have faith.

Here's the second question for you to wrestle with: *Am I open to everything God has for me?* That means any and all of the gifts that the Holy Spirit may want to pour out through your life to further extend God's Kingdom.[34] It's okay to ask God to help you grow in both your desire and your trust.[35]

Think about the audacity it takes to want to pick and choose the gifts of the Holy Spirit. *"Yes, I'd like the gift of faith, but the working of miracles sounds a bit frightening. No thanks on that one."* When we surrender to Christ, it means just that: *surrender.* It means we put him in charge and do as he directs. We've been crucified with him, and we belong to him. From this point forward, we're called to surrender our bodies as living sacrifices. This is the key to a full and complete life in Christ. And, yes, it takes courage, but God will help us if we ask him. As we surrender ourselves, the Holy Spirit is freed up to fill every part of our lives. Then we will be transformed, by the renewing of our minds, and we'll be able to discern God's will for us, which is good, pleasing, and perfect.[36]

Being continually filled with the Holy Spirit doesn't mean the journey will be easy. In fact, we can expect trouble;[37] but we also know that God will never leave us or forsake us.[38] He will continually lead us in triumph,[39] and he will give us abundant life[40] in the power of the Holy Spirit.

Here is a daily prayer to help you to surrender your heart to God alone:

> *Lord, make me hungry to know you*
> *more and to surrender every part of my*
> *life to you. Please help me to be open to*
> *everything you want to do in me and*
> *with me. I want to trust that your grace is*
> *sufficient for me and will equip me with*
> *everything I need in order to do your will.*
> *Amen.*

As you pursue the continual, ongoing filling of the Holy Spirit, have faith in God's promise that "he has filled the hungry with good things."[41]

AWAKENING TO OUR CALLING: GO AND MAKE DISCIPLES

Therefore go and make disciples of all nations, baptizing them
in the name of the Father and of the Son and of the Holy Spirit,
and teaching them to obey everything I have commanded you.
And surely I am with you always, to the very end of the age.

MATTHEW 28:19-20

GOD CREATED EVERY person on earth to be in an intimate, loving relationship with him, but we rebelled and wandered. Still, because God loves us so much, he sent his Son to rescue us from our sin—through Jesus, he made a way for everyone to come back into a right relationship with him.[1] That is the heart of the gospel, the good news of Jesus Christ.

God wants us to care about what he cares about. And his greatest desire is the redemption of the people he created. He wants his lost children found! He wants everyone to be reconciled to him. Nothing matters more to God; the Cross proves that.

Jesus came to earth with a straightforward mission: "to

seek and to save the lost."[2] And now he has passed this calling on to us: "As the Father has sent me, I am sending you."[3]

This is our mission. This is our main purpose for living on earth. When we repent and put our faith in Jesus Christ, God's love in our hearts inspires and motivates us to "*go* and make disciples of all nations."[4]

We are called to follow in Jesus' footsteps by spreading God's love and sharing his plan of salvation. Scripture makes the urgency of our mission very clear. At stake is the eternal destiny of people's souls.

As I've grown in my relationship with God, the Holy Spirit has given me a greater love for Jesus Christ and an increasing concern for the salvation of others. Just as Jesus laid down his life in obedience to his Father's will, I have a deep desire to devote my life to sharing the good news of God's grace.[5] Like the apostle Paul, "my only aim is to finish the race and complete the task the Lord Jesus has given me—the task of testifying to the good news of God's grace."[6]

One thing is certain: God's plan cannot be thwarted. It will succeed. "His intent [is] that now, through the church, the manifold wisdom of God should be made known to the rulers and authorities in the heavenly realms, according to his eternal purpose that he accomplished in Christ Jesus our Lord."[7]

What a privilege and joy it is to show our love for Jesus by going into the world to make more disciples.[8] Furthermore, in doing this, we glorify God by completing the work he has given us to do.[9]

How does Jesus want us to represent him? Simply put, he wants us to do the same things he did when he was on earth:

- He sought out and saved the lost. He lived and walked among the people. He went into people's homes and ate and laughed and cried with them. He listened to them, heard the cry of their hearts, and felt their pain.
- He explained to people what God's Kingdom is like, gave them great hope, and encouraged their hearts.
- He had a particular concern for people with broken hearts. He had a deep compassion for people who were grieving the death of a loved one or who were struggling and had been beaten down by life.
- He freed people whose lives were being ruined by unforgiveness and bitterness.
- He offered great hope and a redeemed lifestyle to people who had made, or were making, bad decisions in life.
- He prayed for people and healed them of their diseases and sicknesses. And he cast out demons from people.

After Jesus had lived with his disciples for a while, teaching them and showing them how to bring the Kingdom of God to bear in the world, he sent out the twelve disciples with clear instructions: *Go* and show people what the Kingdom of God is like. They were to be out among the people, staying in their homes, eating their food, healing the sick, and casting out demons. Their mission was to set people free from captivity and bring light into their darkness. Jesus sent his disciples ahead of him, to the places where he would later visit.

That essential mission has never changed. Now it's our turn to answer the call to action and to follow where Christ leads. Above all, he wants us to *go*—to go where the people are. It may feel a bit uncomfortable at times. We may be called to go places we never would have gone on our own. We may experience some internal conflict, because our natural tendency, our default mode, is to settle. We're more inclined to seek the path of ease and comfort. And yet, at the heart of the gospel, Jesus came from the comfort and glory of heaven to live and die in a broken world, in order to rescue us. When we come to faith in Christ, we become part of the church—his body on earth—and he calls us to lay down our lives, as well as the things we want, in order to carry on his rescue mission. Thankfully, for whatever God calls us to do, he also equips us and sustains us.

When I completed my college studies, I sensed that God wanted me to continue with my career plan to work in the banking industry. My banking and finance degree had been sponsored by a major international bank, and now I had an offer to work in the City of London. Oftentimes, I've found, people think that when God says, "Go," he's asking us to pack up and move to some exotic or foreign location. And though it's certainly true that God may move us to different places in our lives (as he has done several times with Jeannie and me), it's also quite likely he is calling us to *go* right where we are. You see, the essence of "going" is being sent—and that is a mind-set as much as it is a mission.

Regardless of our location or vocation, God desires for us to go into all the world for the purpose of spreading the gospel. So even if the extent of our going is simply to reach our families, neighbors, friends, and coworkers, we're following our mission as long as we "have the mind of Christ" to seek and to save the lost and to bring the good news of salvation to everyone in our midst.[10] And as we keep our minds focused on this goal, we become more flexible and available for God to send or redirect us where he wants us to go.

ETERNAL DESTINY

Jesus gave us two basic commands: "Love God and other people" and "Go and make disciples of all nations."[11] As we love God, a new love, compassion, and concern for other people will grow in our hearts. We will want to help them, and we will be desperately concerned for their eternal destiny.

Over the years, the more I've considered the possible fate of my friends, relatives, neighbors, and colleagues, the more I've found my heart burdened for them. I have to admit that I've often wrestled with the question of how a loving God could allow people to go to hell. Fortunately, others much wiser than I have struggled with the same thoughts. For example, C. S. Lewis writes, "There is no doctrine which I would more willingly remove from Christianity than this [i.e., hell], if it lay in my power. But it has the full support of Scripture and, specially, of Our Lord's own words; it has always been held by Christendom; and it has the support of reason."[12]

Regrettably, we've reached a place in our society where people don't want to hear about hell. It's uncomfortable and not politically correct. But regardless of how we feel about hell, we must ask, "Is it true?" Was Jesus telling the truth when he warned people about eternal judgment? If so, what effect does it have on how we live our lives? If we know the end of the story and other people don't, I think it's fair to say we have an obligation to tell them about it—not as a means of passing judgment on them, but out of genuine concern and compassion for their lives and their destiny.

If a blind man were about to walk off the edge of a cliff, how hard would you try to persuade him to change his course? And if he was *convinced* he was on the right path, how much more persuasive and persistent would you be?

That doesn't mean we go around telling people they're going to hell. That is a definite nonstarter these days. But the thought that someone might wind up in hell should motivate us to take action to prevent it from happening. If we're convinced that hell is real, let's do everything we can to make sure nobody ends up there. That's one reason why we go and share the gospel.

Another motivation to go and to lay down our lives to spread the news of Jesus Christ is that it brings us a sense of fulfillment. God created us to love him and glorify him. And we glorify God by completing the work he has prepared for us to do.[13] When we're in the "sweet spot" of God's will for our lives, we experience his peace in a special way. As we seek first his Kingdom and his righteousness, everything else follows along.[14]

PREPARING TO GO

The best way we can prepare ourselves to "go into all the world"[15] is by spending as much time as we can in the presence of God. That's what the disciples did. They walked with Jesus day by day, watching what he did and hearing what he said, and then they went out and did likewise. Even after Jesus ascended to heaven, what stood out in the lives of his disciples was their close association with him. Here's an example:

> The members of the council were amazed when they saw the boldness of Peter and John, for they could see that they were ordinary men with no special training in the Scriptures. They also recognized them as men who had been with Jesus.[16]

We often feel as if we're unprepared to share the gospel because we think we need to have all the answers. But Jesus tells us simply to *go* and to rely on his provision.[17] After all, when we come to faith in Jesus, our old selves are crucified with him, and it is Christ living in us that the world should now see.[18] Moreover, the apostle Paul says that we "reflect the glory of the Lord," and that the Lord "makes us more and more like him as we are changed into his glorious image."[19] This transformation is carried out by the Holy Spirit, who changes us from within.

As we die to ourselves and live only for God's plan, the life of Christ within us shines through more and more.[20] This is what Jesus meant when he said, "If you abide in me, and my words abide in you, ask whatever you wish, and it will be done for you. By this my Father is glorified, that you bear much fruit and so prove to be my disciples."[21]

GO WITH WHAT YOU'VE SEEN AND HEARD

In Acts 3, as Peter and John are going into the Temple, they encounter a beggar who has been disabled for more than forty years.[22] After Peter heals the man in Jesus' name, the city is in an uproar, and Peter and John are dragged before the religious leaders to account for what happened. In this story, we find some important details that should inform and encourage our calling to share the gospel.

First of all, the success of our mission has nothing to do with our own power or piety—it is all about what *Jesus* has done.

All the people were astonished and came running to them. . . . When Peter saw this, he said to them: "Fellow Israelites, why does this surprise you? Why do you stare at us as if by our own power or godliness we had made this man walk?"[23]

. . . [Peter said,] "Salvation is found in no one else, for there is no other name under heaven given to mankind by which we must be saved."[24]

When they saw the courage of Peter and John and realized that they were unschooled, ordinary men, they were astonished and they took note that these men had been with Jesus.[25]

Secondly, our role in the work of the gospel is simply to go and testify to what we have seen and heard. In the case of Peter and John, the religious leaders said to them, "Look, unless you stop speaking about this person Jesus Christ, you're going to end up like he did—nailed to a cross."[26] And the two disciples replied, "How can we not speak about what we have seen and heard?"[27] Later, John opens his first letter to the church with similar words:

> We proclaim to you the one who existed from the beginning, whom we have heard and seen. We saw him with our own eyes and touched him with our own hands. He is the Word of life. This one who is life itself was revealed to us, and we have seen him. And now we testify and proclaim to you that he is the one who is eternal life. . . . We proclaim to you what we ourselves have actually seen and heard.[28]

GO WHERE GOD SENDS YOU: CHANGING DIRECTION

In my life, there have been some dramatic changes in direction, by which God redirected me to follow his will. Perhaps the most significant occurred when Jeannie and I were living in London. My vision was to serve God there and continue doing ministry work, and I committed to stay in London until Jesus came back or I went to be with him. I had no desire to work or serve overseas, and when the COO of the bank called me into his office one day and asked me to go to New York to launch a global product, I quickly said no. I had been asked to go abroad before and had turned down the offers because I believed God wanted me in London. Little did I know that God was preparing me for a change.

It started with a godly discontentment. I was experiencing a vibrant relationship with the Lord, but I sensed he had something *more* for me. I just assumed it would be "something more" in London.

Not long after this, a woman with a prophetic gifting came to our church. She prayed for the other two pastors, and when she got to me, she said she felt that God was going to send me overseas to lead missionary teams.

I'm a bit slow, and probably stubborn, when it comes to hearing God's voice, so when Jeannie and I left the service, we did not begin to plan or dream what this overseas opportunity might be. Instead, I turned to Jeannie and said, "Well, she got that one wrong, didn't she!"

A short while after that service, and completely unrelated in my mind at the time, we sold our house and started to rent. I had very practical reasons for this decision (to pay off our mortgage, release capital, and get a home where we could park our car), but looking back, I can see that God was gently loosening my grip on the things that were blocking me from hearing his voice.

Despite my initial resistance to an overseas placement with the bank, the COO persisted.

"You can stay in the UK if you want," he said, "but we really think this is a fantastic opportunity for you. Go away and think about it, and give me your answer in forty-eight hours."

I still felt that my answer was a clear *no*, but I thought I should consult with several family members and close friends and ask them to pray about the offer. Their feedback was all in the direction of our going, but I remained unconvinced. On the day of decision, I told Jeannie I still wasn't sure, but that my inclination was to say no. Jeannie, however, surprised me with some news.

"Your mum rang last night while you were at the pastors meeting, and she has 'a word' for you."

Well, I know enough that when your mum has a word for you, it's wise to take notice!

Jeannie told me that the word my mum had for me was from Genesis 24: "This is from the Lord . . . and Rebekah didn't tarry!"

I knew my mum didn't want me to move overseas, yet she was being obedient to pass along a message from the Lord that I should go. That was very powerful. It seemed I was the only person who wasn't seeing the move to the United States as being God's will for us. But with the word from my mum, I became convinced and decided the answer would be *yes*.

Having now made the decision to go, I was amazed by how God confirmed that he was indeed directing this major move for my family and me.

On most days, I cycled into work, but because I was going straight from work that night to lead an Alpha course,

I decided to take the Tube (the London Underground) to work. To grasp the significance of what I'm about to share, you need to realize that it's extremely rare to meet anyone you know on the Tube because of traffic volume and timing. However, as I got on the Tube that morning, I found myself sitting next to a guy I had met the previous week in a sports club. I told him about the decision I had just made to move to New York, and he responded by saying he had worked in Manhattan for ten years.

When I got back on the Tube that night after work, I met a guy who was attending the Alpha course I was leading (there were only about thirty people in the course), and he had also worked in Manhattan for many years.

As I've already mentioned, meeting one person you know on the Tube is quite unusual. But to meet *two* people you know on separate trips inside of the same day is unheard of. That the first person had worked in Manhattan was incredible. To find out that the second person had also worked in Manhattan was mind-boggling. That this all happened on the day I had finally agreed to move to work in Manhattan is, I suggest, a true miracle!

So, does God guide the lives of his children? When I ponder that question, I always come back to this remarkable period in my life.

God is able to change the course of our lives to accomplish his will through us. Our job is simply to *believe* and to keep our hearts in love with Jesus, being willing and ready to obey his will and go.

GO AND ALLOW THE HOLY SPIRIT TO DO HIS WORK

To further underscore the truth that our job is simply to *go* and that the Holy Spirit will do the heavy lifting, let me tell you a wonderful story I heard not long ago.

A young woman named Susan had committed her life to obey God's commands to love other people and to go and make disciples of all nations. While attending college in Manhattan, she made friends with a brilliant young Chinese student named Lin.

Lin had been brought up as an atheist in a major city in China, and her father was a senior member of the Communist party. To further develop Lin's brilliant mind and her education, she was sent to the United States to complete a PhD in Western capitalism and Christianity. In order to research her thesis, she had to analyze both topics and find their weaknesses. Thus, when Susan invited Lin to an Alpha course, explaining it was about Jesus and his teaching, Lin was pleased to accept the invitation, knowing it would provide information for her studies.

Lin was an attentive student, listening well and taking lots of notes. After every Alpha session, she called her mother in China and explained what she had learned. She discussed who Jesus is, why he died on the cross, the significance of his resurrection, and how we can be sure about our faith in him. Everything seemed to be going according to plan until around week six of the course, when Lin's mother replied, "On the basis of what you've been telling me, Lin, I've decided to commit my life to Christ!"

Lin was horrified and angry at this news because she didn't see what her mother had responded to. Still, she finished the course and then decided to attend the next one as well. During the second Alpha course, Lin also came to faith in Jesus, and together with her mother, she was baptized in a Baptist church in Manhattan.

As brilliant as she is, Lin could have gone into the corporate world and earned a huge salary. However, she now knew she had been entrusted with the message of eternal life through Jesus Christ. And though her own eternal destiny was secure, she knew that millions of her countrymen and women were without Christ and without hope. Together with her mother, Lin did a very smart thing. She is now back in China, sharing the wonderful news of Jesus Christ with her family, friends, and acquaintances.

GO—MAKING THE MOST OF LIFE'S CIRCUMSTANCES

At an Alpha event not long ago, I had the privilege of meeting Nick Vujicic. Nick, who is now in his early thirties, was born without any arms or legs. When he was ten, he contemplated suicide (by drowning himself in the bathtub), but he stopped when he thought about the pain it would cause his parents. Nick came to faith in Jesus as a teenager, and with the encouragement of a janitor at his high school, he soon started speaking to groups about his faith and overcoming adversity.[29] He now reaches millions of people as he shares about the living hope he has in Jesus Christ.

Nick exudes the love, joy, and peace of the Lord. He is

clearly at ease with his life, despite his challenges, and has a wonderful way of helping people relax in his presence. When you meet him, the first thing he asks for is a hug. I was fascinated to hear him speak about the living hope within him.

Two things in particular struck me in what Nick shared. First, he said, "I can't wait for heaven!" And second, "When we get to heaven, God will ask us who we brought with us."

In line with Scripture, Nick has a heavenly perspective, setting his heart and mind "on things above."[30] And yet he knows that God has a purpose for his life on earth. Although the doctors can't explain why Nick was born without limbs, he believes God permitted it so that he can lead millions to Christ. Rather than taking offense at the life he has on earth, he is using it to glorify God and to complete the work prepared for him to do.[31]

Nick has tremendous purpose in his life now—and an incredible inheritance awaiting him in heaven that he will enjoy throughout eternity. I pray that we can follow Nick's example by living our lives on earth to glorify God by completing the work he has given us to do.[32] As I remember my days as a runner, I pray that we all will run a great race in our relatively short dash through life on this earth.

GO AND DRIVE OUT THE DARKNESS

Scripture tells us that our battle is not against flesh and blood, but against the spiritual forces of darkness and wickedness in the heavenly realms—the unseen spiritual world that is all around us.[33] This is the realm that Satan uses to blind the eyes of unbelievers and keep them from seeing the glorious gospel of Jesus Christ. Have you ever noticed that you can speak to some people about God until you're blue in the face, using the perfect stories and apologetic arguments, but they still don't understand what you're talking about? They can't see because the spiritual forces of darkness have blinded them.

Do you ever ponder, as I do, why we tend to self-destruct from time to time? We break relationships, battle addictions, and hurt ourselves and others. Scripture teaches that this happens because we pursue selfish desires that harm us, damage other people, and corrupt the whole of creation.[34] The good news is that Jesus offers us forgiveness and healing for our broken hearts, release from our bondage to sin, sight for our blinded eyes, and freedom from oppression by Satan.[35]

So, how do we deal with the spiritual forces of darkness that are keeping people from seeing the Good News of Jesus Christ?

The answer, I believe, is very simple. How do you drive darkness out of a room? Turn on the light. In fact, if you think about it, there's no such thing as darkness. There's only light and the absence of light. With that in mind, watch as Jesus gives us the key to driving out the evil spirits that are blinding people's hearts and destroying their lives.[36]

In Luke 9:1-6, Jesus sends his twelve disciples out to proclaim the Kingdom of God and heal the sick. Now, at the beginning of Luke 10, he gives the same instructions, only this time it is to seventy-two disciples. Once again, the call to action is unequivocal: "Go!"

When the disciples return to Jesus with a report that even the demons submitted to them in his name,[37] he says something very interesting: "I saw Satan fall like lightning from heaven."[38] It's as if the disciples, in taking the light of the gospel out into the world, *zapped* the prince of darkness.

I believe this is a very strategic statement—in fact, it's the key to driving back the forces of darkness that are ever seeking to bring blindness, death, and destruction to God's creation and, in particular, to humankind.

So, how does the "Go!" model change the spiritual atmosphere and help people to see the Kingdom of God? It has to do with God's purpose for the church—that is, the body of Christ in the world today:

> God's purpose in all this was to use the church
> to display his wisdom in its rich variety to all the
> unseen rulers and authorities in the heavenly places.
> This was his eternal plan, which he carried out
> through Christ Jesus our Lord.[39]

The key question is this: Where does the spiritual light come from to drive out the forces of darkness? *From people who know and are following Christ!*[40]

> Here's another way to put it: You're here to be light,
> bringing out the God-colors in the world. God is not
> a secret to be kept. We're going public with this, as
> public as a city on a hill. If I make you light-bearers,

you don't think I'm going to hide you under a
bucket, do you? I'm putting you on a light stand.
Now that I've put you there on a hilltop, on a light
stand—shine! Keep open house; be generous with
your lives. By opening up to others, you'll prompt
people to open up with God, this generous Father
in heaven.[41]

It has always been God's plan to work through the church to
usher in his Kingdom on earth. God gives us, his followers,
the opportunity to join with him in the work he is doing.
God has caused his light to shine in our hearts,[42] and Jesus
has told us that we are now the light of the world.[43] It is God's
light in us that drives out the darkness in the heavenly realms.

That's why it's so important for us to *go*. We carry the
presence of God with us. And, for people to experience
God's presence, we need to be with them! Through us, God
is spreading the fragrance of Jesus Christ in our families,
neighborhoods, workplaces, and wherever we go.[44]

So, what are we waiting for? We have the filling of the
Holy Spirit available to us and the light of God shining in
our hearts. All we need is obedience to make our faith complete and spread the Kingdom of God. As my friend Jackson
Senyonga has said, "The Kingdom of God is motion acti-
vated." Like an automatic door, it doesn't open until you
move forward. Things won't start to happen in your life until
you step out in obedience to Christ. I believe Jesus wants all
his followers to live lives that are dependent on his grace,

mercy, and guidance. I don't know exactly what that means for you in practical terms, but it will require you to walk by faith. As I have discovered, there will be times when we have to trust God even when things don't work out as we had planned. We must keep going into all the world with the gospel, even when the way ahead seems impossible. "For everyone born of God overcomes the world. This is the victory that has overcome the world, even our faith."[45]

4

AWAKENING TO BROKENNESS

*The righteous cry out, and the LORD hears them; he delivers
them from all their troubles. The LORD is close to the
brokenhearted and saves those who are crushed in spirit.*

PSALM 34:17-18

THE WORLD IS BROKEN. There's no two ways about it. As we
answer the call to *go*, we bring restoration and wholeness to
people who are suffering the effects of brokenness.

I intentionally put this chapter right here in the middle
of everything, because that's how we so often experience brokenness. It steps in at the most inopportune moments and
takes us to our knees—both literally and figuratively.

Whether that brokenness comes as a result of our stepping
back into the miry clay from which we were rescued,[1] or a
circumstance beyond our control—tragedy, disappointment,
betrayal, sickness, sorrow—brokenness is not something we
simply step around and then continue merrily on our way.

Brokenness and suffering are issues we must confront in our own lives and in the lives of everyone around us. We cannot escape the consequences of life's painful experiences. They mark us permanently. But it is out of our pain and our brokenness that true wholeness can emerge. That's the hope we have for ourselves. That's the hope we can extend to others. Not that we can avoid suffering. But that God is a master at mosaic—creating something beautiful from all the broken pieces.

PERSONAL TRAGEDY AND ETERNITY

There's something about affliction that purifies our motives.[2] I know from firsthand experience that God can uniquely use significant amounts of pain to change our viewpoint on life.[3] Through my pain, eternity has become very clear to me, and I find I now have a deep passion for souls and a longing for heaven and for Jesus' return. We have such a very short time in this age, and then, depending on whether we accept or reject Jesus Christ, we pass either into God's presence or apart from him. We get to heaven only through Jesus Christ and his substitutional and redemptive death on the cross. It's only because he took the punishment that we deserve. God has also prepared specific work for each one of us to complete while we're on earth.[4]

God enabled me to come to this realization through the passing of close family members: my younger son, Alex, in 2005, followed two months later by the death of my sister, Jax. Scripture says that God has "set eternity in the human heart,"[5] and I believe it is often brokenness that releases this understanding.

Alex was seventeen when he passed away. He committed suicide after a series of events that began with his taking a drug and becoming delusional. Then it freaked him out when a Wiccan he encountered put a curse on him. This was a period in our lives when it seemed as if evil had been released on our household.

The suicide of a child is said to be the worst pain a person can endure—right up there with being tortured in prison. Your emotions, mind, body, and spirit are all deeply affected. You can never get away from the pain; it's with you 24-7. Although sleep gives some respite, the pain often catches up with you even there. Jeannie and I would often wake up crying. If I was awake in the night, I would hear her crying out in her sleep. If I woke her up, she would be out of her subconscious nightmare and back into her conscious nightmare. Nine years later, she still cries out in her sleep.

Jeannie suffered terribly with Alex's suicide and the way that it happened. Alex was our youngest, and his mother adored him. They were very close, and Jeannie was especially sensitive to the fact that Alex was having to adjust to a new high school in a foreign land and culture.

Jeannie and I had been through a lot already, serving God together in some very difficult circumstances over the previous twenty-four years. She had always been a wonderfully loyal wife to me and had a sweet walk with the Lord. But Alex's suicide was more than her faith could cope with, and the shock and pain soon turned to anger—and then to hatred. It was horrible. She hated and blamed herself, me, and God.

One of the giant effects of suicide is *blame*. If you let it, it will crush you. And that's what happened to Jeannie. She desperately tried to rewind our lives to avoid that horrible night. Over and over, she rehearsed the previous five years and our decision to come to America and then to move to Chicago.

Why did we send Alex to such a big school where he must have suffered so much?

Why didn't we recognize the warning signs?

Why didn't we do more?

On and on and on she went, trying to bring Alex back. In her grief, she was close to losing her mind, and one night she ran out the back door in her nightgown, and off into the night—trying to get away from the boundless pain and terror of the whole thing. Fortunately, I spotted her, and my training as a runner came in handy as I managed to catch her before she ran out into the road.

Out of concern that she might try to take her own life, I took her to the hospital for a preadmission psychiatric evaluation. At the last minute, I realized that being with other psychiatric patients might have finished her off, and I managed to persuade the doctors that we could look after her at home.

All this time, Jeannie had been saying, "I wish I had never been born." This is a step beyond "I wish I could die." The pain and horror had by now outweighed anything positive she had previously experienced in her life—and she'd had

GERARD LONG || 49

some very good memories—and she had nowhere to go. After hating God for a time because of what had happened to Alex, she now decided he didn't exist. She lost her faith and was in utter darkness.

Four months after that terrible night, the pain became too much for Jeannie's body, and her intestines knotted up. She awoke one morning in excruciating pain, and it was all I could do to hold myself together enough to get her to the hospital. We raced her into the emergency room, and after several hours of tests, the doctors determined that she needed lifesaving surgery.

Was this it? Was God going to grant Jeannie her wish for release from this life?

As she was about to be wheeled into surgery, I really thought it might be the last time I saw my precious wife this side of heaven. She saw it on my face, and she was thinking along the same lines. But then she beckoned me to come close to her and in a weak voice said, "Gerard, you know, I really do want to live!"

Those were days of incredible pain and suffering. On top of my own shattered heart, I was trying to love and take care of Jeannie when all she returned to me was hatred and anger. (She blamed me for decisions she felt may have contributed to Alex's suicide.) Meanwhile, I was wrestling with God over the whole thing. Not only that, but our daughter, Rebecca, was grappling with her own grief, and our other son, Ben, was facing everything on his own back in London.

By God's grace, my faith held firm, and I ran as hard as

I could into God. He was my refuge from the storm.[6] His grace, and only his grace, sustained me in this time of utter brokenness. In particular, the Bible and the Holy Spirit provided food for my hungry heart and comfort for my wounded soul.[7] The Lord provided for me in many amazing ways. For example, for the first twelve months after Alex passed away, an anonymous person sent me a postcard every day with "Love" on one side and a Scripture passage on the other.

Most evenings, I would go up to bed, depleted and exhausted, around 9:30, only to awaken around 2:00 a.m. In those early morning hours, I would rise, make myself a cup of tea, and pour out my heart to God in prayer. Often, I wept deeply from the bottom of my soul until I had no more tears to shed, listening for the still, small voice of the Holy Spirit to comfort me, wash me, and cleanse me.[8] I also pored over Scripture time and again, consuming it, clinging to God's promises, and for a time, asking the big question: *WHY?* In the midst of my grief, I was emboldened and encouraged by these Scriptures:

> Let us therefore come boldly to the throne of grace, that we may obtain mercy and find grace to help in time of need.[9]

> Those who wait on the LORD shall renew their strength; they shall mount up with wings like eagles, they shall run and not be weary, they shall walk and not faint.[10]

You shall hide them in the secret place of Your
presence from the plots of man; You shall keep them
secretly in a pavilion from the strife of tongues.[11]

Despite my grief, or perhaps because of it, these were times
of the most intimate fellowship with God I'd ever had. His
presence offered incredible solace, and I can remember at
least one occasion when I distinctly sensed that Jesus was
weeping with me. I realized then how much God sees and
feels the pain we go through on earth. Sometimes we think
he is far removed from our suffering, but he isn't. His heart
breaks with ours; he weeps with us; he sees it all and feels it
all, I'm convinced.

These were also days of deep revelation for me. I saw the
truth in Scripture at a new level and understood far more of
God's heart and purpose for me and his church. This may be
hard for some to understand (and I'm not in any way suggest-
ing that everyone who suffers loss should feel this way), but I
began to realize that my suffering was a tremendous privilege.
"For it has been granted to you on behalf of Christ not only
to believe in him, but also to suffer for him."[12] Through my
utter brokenness, God revealed himself to me: "It was good
for me to be afflicted so that I might learn your decrees."[13]

The most powerful revelation I received at this time was
an acute awareness of our eternal destiny. Through my broken
heart, a deep appreciation for eternity had now been released.

This revelation of eternity came as I wrestled with God
over why he had allowed Satan to inflict so much evil on my

family. Jeannie had already decided she could not believe in God because of what had happened to Alex, but I clung to what I read in Scripture: that God is good all the time.[14] He must have a reason for permitting Satan to "sift" us—similar to Job and Peter![15]

Here's what I saw: Alex had made a terrible mistake, but he had previously put his faith in Jesus Christ. I knew he was in heaven. We are going to see him again, and our relationship with him will be that much greater through eternity because of what we've lost.[16] Yes, our hearts are broken, and yes, we desperately miss Alex, but God will more than make it up to us. Our relationship with Alex will be a hundredfold better throughout eternity because of laying our lives down now to God's will for us. I got it. I saw it! When I viewed things just from the world's perspective, I could make no sense of Alex's suicide. But when I viewed what had happened from an eternal perspective, everything changed. God was and is using our brokenness for his eternal purposes—and in particular, that many more precious souls will be in heaven throughout eternity, through faith in Jesus Christ. God has compensated for our pain and loss by revealing himself to us now, and we know we have a glorious inheritance awaiting us in heaven.

For our light and momentary troubles are achieving
for us an eternal glory that far outweighs them all.
So we fix our eyes not on what is seen, but on what
is unseen, since what is seen is temporary, but what
is unseen is eternal.[17]

Praise be to the God and Father of our Lord Jesus
Christ! In his great mercy he has given us new birth
into a living hope through the resurrection of Jesus
Christ from the dead, and into an inheritance that
can never perish, spoil or fade. This inheritance is
kept in heaven for you.[18]

Thankfully, I saw this truth early on, and it helped me persevere through the next two years while Jeannie lost her faith.
This was a very painful season, and frankly, it was only by
God's grace that our marriage survived. For Jeannie, the journey to this revelation has taken eight years, and even now
she struggles from time to time with the thought that God
could have permitted Alex's suicide for a higher eternal purpose.[19] Jeannie is currently writing her own book describing
her journey through the Valley of Baca (weeping), and it will
be very powerful and helpful to anyone who has suffered any
form of loss.

Just two months after Alex passed away, my sister, Jax,
died suddenly of cancer. As her life slipped away, I raced over
to the UK to try to see her one last time before she died. I was
so glad she hung on until I could get there. Within an hour
of my arrival, she passed into glory. For some time, Jax had
lain semiconscious in her hospital bed with only the whites of
her eyes showing. But just before she died, she suddenly was
focused and staring ahead. My mother, a wonderfully godly
lady, said, "She is seeing Jesus." And then Jax was gone. She
was fifty-three years old.

In 2010, my brother Will contracted a very aggressive form of cancer, and his health deteriorated rapidly. Of course, we cried out to the Lord for healing, but the Lord chose to take Will at age fifty-four. I'm grateful that my mum and my other brother, Kim, and I were able to travel to France to be with Will for three days before he breathed his last breath and went to be with Jesus, joining that "great cloud of witnesses."[20] It was a special time of togetherness, and it was amazing to speak with Will just before he passed away. I asked him to give Jesus, Alex, our dad, and Jax a big hug from me. Will ran a good race, and it was wonderful to hear the chief doctor say to us that, in all his time in medicine, he had never seen anyone with such peace as Will had, even though he knew he would soon die.

I'll never forget what happened as we sat with Will and he passed into glory. About thirty seconds after exhaling his last breath, he suddenly blew out another burst of air. This wasn't a normal breath, because he hadn't breathed in. I believe this was his spirit leaving his body to be with God in heaven.

The brokenness that came from these and other losses is another story. The pain and hurt are difficult to even begin to capture, but I share them with you now because they have been instrumental in convincing me how fragile and temporary life on earth really is. They have served to awaken me to God's presence and to shift my vision to eternity. And though I'm still learning and growing from these experiences, I believe that one of the reasons God has allowed me to go through such loss is so that I can sound a trumpet blast, a wake-up call, to the church to the urgency of our mission.

COMING BACK FROM THE BRINK

For two years or so after Alex's suicide, many areas of my life were very difficult. During this time, my heart was broken from the loss of both Alex and Jax; Jeannie had lost her faith and hated God, herself, and me; and I was still trying to deliver on my responsibilities at work. I know without a shadow of a doubt that it was only with God's strength that I was able to keep going, to continue to love Jeannie, and to hold our marriage together. I know this because, on at least two occasions, I told God, "I can't do this anymore. If you want me to continue, you must give me the strength." Amazingly, in both instances, the next day I found I had fresh love and strength to keep going! Where did this love and strength come from? It came directly from the throne of grace.[21]

God's grace enables us to triumph in any and every situation, and what God builds into us becomes a fragrant aroma revealing Jesus through our lives.[22] He causes us to shine ever brighter for him in a dark and broken world.[23] His work in our lives draws others toward us and provides us with opportunities to tell people what God has accomplished.

Is it hard for you to find the time and motivation to pray and spend time in God's presence? This is not surprising, because Satan, the world, and our flesh are all working against us. I have found that I must really exercise my will in order to spend more time in God's Word and in prayer.

My time with God is very simple. It's like meeting a friend. I listen for the voice of the Holy Spirit, and I practice a variety of personal disciplines, including thanksgiving, silence, praise and worship, memorizing Scripture, and presenting requests in line with what I know to be God's will, such as, "Holy Spirit, please fill me afresh today."

George Müller once wrote, "I saw more clearly than ever that the first great and primary business to which I ought to attend every day was, to have my soul happy in the Lord."[24] In my time with the Lord, I always look to experience his joy, which gives me strength and encouragement for the day.[25]

Scripture talks about the eyes of the heart.[26] These are "spiritual eyes" that allow us to see and understand the Kingdom of God. In the Old Testament, we see glimpses of God's eternal Kingdom and purpose breaking through into the natural realm. For example, even though Joseph had endured terrible treatment at the hands of his brothers, he was willing to forgive them. He said, "You intended to harm me, but God intended it for good to accomplish what is now being done, the saving of many lives."[27] Joseph could see that God had been working a higher, eternal plan that redeemed all that Joseph had suffered. Are you able to see the eternal plan behind the things you have suffered in your life? If not, are you able to trust God that there is one?

Another good example of the eyes of faith seeing God's bigger, eternal plan occurs in 2 Kings 6:8-17, when the Arameans attack Israel. The prophet Elisha gives the king of Israel supernatural "insider information" that enables the king to thwart the attacks. This infuriates the king of Aram, and he decides to send a "strong force" to capture Elisha. To allay the fears this threat caused Elisha's servant, and to show something of the power of God, Elisha prays, "Open his eyes, LORD, so that he may see."[28] The servant's eyes are opened, and he sees the hills filled with horses and chariots of fire all around Elisha. For a moment, the servant is able to see the cosmic battle taking place in the unseen spiritual realm. Not surprisingly, the Arameans are captured and handed over to the king of Israel.

These stories reassure us that God is still for us, even if we think that everyone and everything is against us. "If God is for us, who can be against us?"[29] "He who is in you is greater than he who is in the world."[30]

As Christ followers, we are engaged in a cosmic battle for the souls of men and women. And we must constantly be on our guard against the schemes of our adversary, the devil, who wants to neutralize us in our service for God and take us out of the battle.[31] Maybe Satan has already done that with you. Maybe you've been terribly disappointed and discouraged by an event in your life, such as bereavement; a broken relationship; or the loss of health, a job, or your life savings. Whatever it is, Satan has managed to outwit and deceive you into thinking that God must not be in control, and must not love you, because of what has happened to you. The truth is, God wants to prepare you for a great work in service to him and his eternal purposes.

If, like me, you've been knocked out of the saddle by

the events of life, please allow me to encourage you to pick yourself up, dust yourself off, and by God's grace get back into the fight! We need you on the front lines helping to take back territory from the enemy.

5

AWAKENING TO ETERNITY

Where there is no vision, the people perish.
PROVERBS 29:18, KJV

Since we consider and look not to the things that are seen
but to the things that are unseen; for the things that are
visible are temporal (brief and fleeting), but the things
that are invisible are deathless and everlasting.
2 CORINTHIANS 4:18, AMP

THE HOLY SPIRIT helps us to understand God's bigger picture of redemption, which is essential to our efforts to spread the good news of the gospel. Compared to eternity, Scripture describes our lives on earth as a breath or a vapor.[1] However, while we are on earth, God has called us to complete a specific mission.[2] To be effective in completing this mission, we're called to live as "foreigners and exiles" on earth.[3] Our faithfulness to this work will be rewarded throughout eternity.[4]

Before unpacking God's specific mission for you and me, it's important to consider how we view ourselves and our lives on earth, because our outlook greatly affects how we live. When I was living for myself, everything revolved around *my* perspective. In pursuit of my selfish desires, I often hurt other people, and my decision making was seriously flawed because I took little or no account of the bigger picture.

The quality of your decisions about how to plan and live your life *here* and *now* depends on how you view the future. Moses summarizes this well in Psalm 90:12: "Teach us to number our days, that we may gain a heart of wisdom." In other words, help us to gain a correct perspective on our earthly lives—in light of eternity—so that we will make wise decisions about how we live today.

When you view your life in the context of eternity, it drastically changes your perspective about this present age.

STORING UP TREASURE IN HEAVEN

If we really believe what Jesus said, that we should store up for ourselves treasure in heaven,[5] and that God will reward us throughout eternity for our faithfulness to his calling here on earth,[6] it only makes sense that we would live for the "things above."[7] The only logical and rational way to live is to give ourselves totally to obeying God's will. Anything else would be foolish! This is how Jesus lived on earth—completing the will of his Father in heaven.[8]

Let me be sure to clarify one thing: We get to heaven *only* by grace, through faith in Jesus Christ, and this is a gift from God.[9] God doesn't promise us rewards as a bribe, but rather as an incentive to encourage us on our life's journey. He wants to do all he can to inspire you and me to come into the fullness of life he has given us in his Son, Jesus Christ. He created us to respond to rewards and prizes.[10] Our ultimate prize is Jesus, and the rewards and treasures of heaven will be the things that God gives us to please Jesus.

Think of the tremendous pleasure of bringing joy and fulfillment to the person you love with all your heart. That will be your joy in heaven—pleasing God and doing his will. And yes, there will be meaningful and fulfilling work to do in heaven as you accomplish God's will for his Kingdom.[11]

Some people think that if we set our hearts and minds on things above,[12] it means we won't be looking for God's Kingdom here on earth. However, I believe the exact opposite is true. When we're freed from the anxieties and worries of earthly life—"the deceitfulness of wealth and the desires for other things," all of which choke out the life of God in us—we can give ourselves fully to producing a crop of righteousness: "some thirty, some sixty, some a hundred times what was sown."[13]

A vision for eternity will profoundly change how we live today.

C. S. LEWIS AND ETERNITY

C. S. Lewis had a wonderful understanding of eternity:

If you read history, you will find that the Christians
who did most for the present world were just
those who thought most of the next. The Apostles
themselves who set on foot the conversion of the
Roman Empire, the great men who built up the

Middle Ages, the English Evangelicals who abolished the Slave Trade, all left their mark on Earth, precisely because their minds were occupied with Heaven. It is since Christians have largely ceased to think of the other world that they have become so ineffective in this. Aim at Heaven and you will get earth "thrown in"; aim at earth and you will get neither.[14]

Most of us find it very difficult to want "Heaven" at all—except in so far as "Heaven" means meeting again our friends who have died. One reason for this difficulty is that we have not been trained: our whole education tends to fix our minds on this world. Another reason is that when the real want for Heaven is present in us, we do not recognize it.[15]

As Lewis indicates, when you live for heaven, you are set free from the allure of this world and can give yourself fully to the will of God. This is real freedom and fullness of life. The Holy Spirit brings this revelation through Scripture, through the renewal of your mind,[16] and sometimes through brokenness. And when you grasp the reality of "his good, pleasing, and perfect will,"[17] you can't help but want to share it with others.

JIM ELLIOT AND ETERNITY

A vision of eternity helps to release the Kingdom of God in and through us as followers of Christ. It means that, whatever the cost, we're willing to give ourselves fully to the will and purpose of God. We will be living sacrifices that God can use for his glory and the advancement of his Kingdom. A profound example of this can be seen in the life of Jim Elliot. Elliot well understood that he could store up for himself treasure in heaven by laying down his life to advance God's Kingdom on earth. He said, "He is no fool who gives what he cannot keep to gain what he cannot lose."[18]

Along with four other young men (some of whom were married with children), Jim Elliot felt God calling him to share the good news of Jesus Christ with the unreached and dangerous Waodani people in the remote jungles of Ecuador. After they made initial contact with the Waodani, the five young men were ruthlessly attacked and slaughtered by the very people they were there to love and serve. Incredibly, Jim's wife, Elisabeth, later returned as a missionary to the same people who had killed her husband. In what could only make sense through the power of the Holy Spirit, many members of the tribe came to faith in Jesus Christ, and two of them even baptized Jim and Elisabeth's daughter.

Some people think that the martyrdom of these five young men was a terrible waste. Certainly, if you assess their lives and deaths simply from the perspective of this world, it was a tragedy that caused tremendous pain and suffering to many people, most notably their families. And yet, when you view the event with the backdrop of eternity, things look very different. Consider, for example, that thousands of other young people have been inspired to go into missions by the sacrifice of Jim Elliot and his friends, and that thousands more precious souls will now be in heaven as a result.

Elisabeth Elliot, along with the other widows and children, experienced a deep intimacy with God because of their pain and suffering. And all the people who suffered due to these men's sacrifice will be rewarded throughout eternity. Think about that . . . eternity goes on *forever*! We would do well to remember this as we decide how much of our lives we are going to surrender to God. The wise will give their all to God. They will hold nothing back. They will become a living sacrifice to see God's Kingdom come and his will done on earth as it is in heaven.[19]

JONATHAN EDWARDS AND ETERNITY

Jonathan Edwards was born in Connecticut in 1703, the only son of eleven children. His father, Timothy Edwards, was a minister, and his mother, Esther Stoddard, was a minister's daughter. Edwards, who entered Yale College in 1716 at the age of thirteen, "is widely acknowledged to be America's most important and original philosophical theologian."[20]

Jonathan Edwards had a significant impact on the development of theology in America, and he had a clear belief and understanding of eternity:

It becomes us to spend this life only as a journey towards heaven, . . . to which we should subordinate all other concerns of life. Why should we labor for, or set our hearts on, anything else, but that which is our proper end and true happiness?[21]

Resolved, to endeavor to obtain for myself as much happiness, in the other world, as I possibly can.[22]

Jesus said, "Do not store up for yourselves treasures on earth, where moths and vermin destroy, and where thieves break in and steal. But store up for yourselves treasures in heaven, where moths and vermin do not destroy, and where thieves do not break in and steal. For where your treasure is, there your heart will be also."[23]

C. T. STUDD AND ETERNITY

When you think about the generations that will follow you, what do you want to leave behind as your legacy to them?

As a young man, C. T. Studd was on the road to success as a graduate of Cambridge University, a world-class cricketer, and heir to a multimillion-dollar estate. But he gave up all of this in order to invest his life in missionary work to China, India, and Africa.[24] He started the Heart of Africa Mission, which became the Worldwide Evangelization Crusade (now WEC International).

Near the end of his life, one of Studd's four daughters came to see him on the mission field. Both father and daughter knew it would be their last visit. The daughter asked if she could have a memento by which to remember her father. C. T. Studd went into his tent and came out a few moments later saying, "I've got nothing left. I've just got my Bible. I've given everything else away."

There were no material possessions to leave to his family, but the spiritual legacy he left behind was of far greater worth. Through his work, thousands, if not millions, of people around the world have found saving faith in Jesus Christ. This was a man who understood his breath of life in terms of eternity. He wisely chose to give his life to what would last for all eternity.

C. T. Studd said, "Some wish to live within the sound of church or chapel bell; I want to run a rescue shop within a yard of hell."[25] He also said, "If Jesus Christ be God and died for me, then no sacrifice can be too great for me to make for Him."[26]

So let me ask you: What is it that you're leaving behind for your children and loved ones? A rich inheritance of material wealth? Or a heritage that will stretch forever into eternity?

6

AWAKENING TO OPPORTUNITY: A BIGGER VISION

Follow me, and I will make you fishers of men.
MATTHEW 4:19, ESV

SHORTLY AFTER JEANNIE AND I were married, we were given a late, monetary wedding gift, which we decided to use for a trip to Israel. We stayed at the YMCA in Tiberias, which turned out to be a beautiful, historic villa set right on the shoreline of the Sea of Galilee. One of the special memories of the trip was watching how the fishermen out on the lake used techniques dating back to the time of Jesus to bring in the day's catch. Jeannie and I were fascinated to see how the men extended a large net between two boats, forming a semicircle in the water, and then thrashed the water with sticks to chase the fish into the net. It was amazing how successful this strategy was.

I've often wondered, in recalling the Tiberias fishermen, what it is that Jesus wants us to understand by his analogy of "fishing for men." Though not a fisherman myself, I know enough about it generally to draw some contrasts between what I've seen of fishing in Britain and the United States and what Jeannie and I observed in Israel.

In America in particular, the classic image of the fisherman is of a lone sportsman, standing knee-deep in a cascading stream, rhythmically casting flies into eddies and along the banks, trying to lure the lunkers out of hiding. This is in line with the ethic of rugged individualism that permeates American culture. But I believe that Jesus wants us to understand and undertake a more collaborative and interactive approach in our fishing for men. I think there's something to be learned from stretching the nets to capture all comers and letting the Lord sort it all out later.

Another important distinction, I believe, is that the fishermen on the Sea of Galilee were in it for a living. It was their calling, their purpose. So perhaps a commercial fishery is a better illustration of what it means to "fish for men" than the picture of the solitary fly-fisher on a secluded stream.

We've looked at the mandate to *go* into all the world to make disciples, but here we must consider an important prerequisite: *We must awaken to our mission and learn how to fish.* Before we can *go*, we must *follow*. That means coming along behind Jesus, staying close, watching, and learning.

Once we understand our unique calling to "fish for people," following the example of Jesus, our perspective will naturally change, and we will begin to live more intentionally for Christ rather than for ourselves. Accepting this truth in our hearts is a crucial step in our becoming better fishers of men. Once we grasp our calling and our mission, it changes our approach to the people God has placed in our lives.

Maybe up until now you've been working out your own plan for your life. Now, however, I hope you see that God has been working in your life for *his* plan. With this knowledge, your approach to life should be, "Lord, show me how to complete the plan you have prepared for me."

After Jesus fed the five thousand, the crowd came to him and asked, "What must we do, to be doing the works of God?"[1] Their question is very powerful, and the answer Jesus gave them is very significant for us today: "This is the work of God, that you believe in him whom he has sent."[2]

Our job as followers of Jesus and as fishers of men is to *believe* (that is, to put our trust) in Jesus, and in his promises, in particular. To believe that he is our Good Shepherd, who guides our lives. To believe that we are the apple of his eye and that nothing and no one can touch our lives without his permission. And even if we make bad decisions and go astray, he is able to rescue us and bring us back on track.

How has God been working in your life to bring you to where you are today?

As I look back over my life, I can clearly see how God has prepared me "for such a time as this."[3] In surrendering my life to Christ and seeing now through eyes of faith, I recognize how God's "good, pleasing and perfect will"[4] has brought me to where I am today. From my family upbringing; five years in a military boarding school; training as an athlete; more than twenty-five years of experience in planning and organizing resources to achieve a common goal with a major international bank; seventeen years pastoring a church in London; and then utter brokenness through the loss of my son Alex, my dad, my sister, and my brother, I can see how God has worked in my life to prepare me for his purpose.

As you look back over your own life, can you see how God has prepared you for the plans he has for you? What gifts, experience, and abilities has he given you? Who are the people in your family and other parts of your life who don't know Christ?

If, like me, you've ignored God's voice at times, neglected his will, and pursued your own selfish desires, know that he is still able to turn your life into something beautiful. The important thing is that you begin walking by faith—starting right now—and seeking after God boldly and courageously through prayer.

CONTINUING ON GOD'S TRACK

My move out of banking began with a similar "godly discontentment" as the one that initiated our move from the UK to the US. About three years after we moved to America, I had a sense that God again had something more for me to do. I'd now had twenty-eight years on an executive program with HSBC and had many opportunities yet ahead, but I sensed that God was finally calling me out of banking.

Over the years, many people had asked me why I wasn't in full-time Christian work. I always told them I was working full-time for the Lord (but I knew what they meant). Now, it seemed, God was indeed calling me out of the marketplace and into vocational ministry.

However, in the process of changing courses in my life, I learned a valuable lesson. Often when God plants a seed of change in our lives, the seed must germinate before the actual change takes place. Where I nearly went wrong was to take matters into my own hands and try to force the move. Thankfully, the Lord rescued me, and I avoided making a real mess of things. By waiting for God's timing, I was able to witness his incredible provision.

During the waiting period, we entered our season of utter brokenness (which I described in chapter 4), and through this, God released in my heart a desperation for saving souls. I had always been concerned for the lost, and doing my part as I saw opportunity, but now there was a fresh urgency to it.

About this time, Jeannie and I received our green cards, granting us permanent residence in the United States. This made the transition much smoother as we could now look to the long term.

The move was triggered when I met with the chairman of Alpha USA for breakfast, and he explained that he had been praying for more than a year for someone with the relevant business planning and organizational skills—and a knowledge and experience of Alpha—to take on the role of chief operating officer.

"Frankly," he said, "I really doubted there was anyone who could meet the criteria."

As he and I spoke, it became clear to me that God had been training me for just such a time as this. Not only had I gained valuable experience while delivering some of the largest organizational changes in the banking industry, but I had also led more than forty Alpha courses in various locations, including our home, churches, the workplace, and a Conservative Club. It seemed ideal to work in a ministry that is all about making disciples of Jesus Christ and saving souls for eternity.

Practically, God used various means of encouragement to move me along the path to my new calling, including some helpful input from the chairman of HSBC. The bank was very kind in allowing me to take an unpaid sabbatical for my first year working for Alpha USA. This was significant, because it let me reach the age of fifty and take an early retirement package. I drew down some of my pension and was able to pay off a piece of my mortgage, which helped me to qualify for a special all-in-one mortgage account with a favorable interest rate. This was a key provision, because in moving out of banking and into the nonprofit sector, I took a 70 percent reduction in salary. But with the lower interest rate, we were able to stay in our home.

I'm convinced that if you will wait for the Lord's timing and the Lord's provision, you will experience the truth that "God will liberally supply (fill to the full) your every need according to His riches in glory in Christ Jesus."[5]

Suffice it to say that I love my work with Alpha, and though the job at times is very challenging, it has been the greatest joy to use the skills and experience I acquired in my banking career to help extend the Kingdom of God, and in particular to spread the gospel to millions of people across America.

WHAT'S IN YOUR HAND?

God has been—and is—working in you to prepare you for such a time as this. He has placed in your hands various gifts, abilities, and experiences—including, perhaps, some brokenness—that you can now use to accomplish the purpose he has set before you.

Consider how God prepared Joseph, Moses, and David for the calling he had on each of their lives. Even Jesus had thirty years of unseen, yet faithful, ministry to his earthly father, Joseph, before emerging in his public ministry.

How has God been equipping *you*?

In preparing to be fishers of men, it's time for us to see through the eyes of faith what God has placed in our hands. The size or volume of the gift is not important. What matters is our faithfulness and willingness to use what God has given us. God gives us what we need, we give him what we have, and he turns it into something beautiful that he can use to further his Kingdom on earth.

One of my favorite examples from Scripture, which powerfully illustrates this point, is the miracle of the feeding of the five thousand that began with a young boy giving to Jesus what he had in his hand: five loaves and two fish.[6]

One day, God will ask each of us what we did with the gifts and talents he gave us. All he expects is that we've been faithful stewards with whatever he has given us. If he's given us a lot, he will expect a lot from us.[7] And we will be rewarded for our faithfulness to his calling.[8]

Here are some ways that you may consider using your unique gifts:

- *Hospitality:* Use your generosity to run an Alpha course or a Bible study in your home, or to bless international students with a place to go for the comforts of home.

- *Intercession:* If you have a particular concern for people and situations, offer the gift of prayer to serve your church by interceding for those in need.

- *Healing:* If you have a calling to pray for sick people, pray diligently and serve your brothers and sisters in Christ in this way.

- *Words of Knowledge:* In praying for people and situations, if you find you have information coming to your mind that could only have been placed there by the Holy Spirit, look for everyday opportunities to pray for people and thereby serve the church.

Perhaps God has placed you in a particular life situation from which he wants to use you:

- *Senior Citizens:* You are in a special position. You may have a lot of spare time because your days working in a profession are over. Perhaps you could use this time to pray for the Kingdom of God to be seen on earth as it is in heaven.

- *Businesspeople:* If your business is successful, watch out, because you are in a precarious position. Money is so easily substituted for trusting Jesus. God has given you finances to help fund the work of the Kingdom. You have the opportunity to make a big impact for the Kingdom of God, but you also need to be careful not to become independent of the Lord. The safest and most fulfilling thing to do with your money is to give it away! Remember, you can't out-give God.

- *Brokenhearted:* Are you in a place of brokenness? Have circumstances in your life given you tremendous pain and driven you toward despair? Perhaps you're grieving the loss of a loved one; maybe your marriage didn't work out as you hoped and now you're living with a very difficult spouse; perhaps your health has failed or you've lost your business or your job and you're facing financial ruin. In spite of all you've been through, Scripture teaches that you're greatly blessed. You may not see it now, but one day you will receive an eternal reward for your faithfulness to the Lord.

"Most assuredly, I say to you, unless a grain of wheat falls into the ground and dies, it remains alone; but if it dies, it produces much grain. He who loves his life will lose it, and he who hates his life in this world will keep it for eternal life."[9]

"These trials will show that your faith is genuine. It is being tested as fire tests and purifies gold—though your faith is far more precious than mere gold. So when your faith remains strong through many trials, it will bring you much praise and glory and honor on the day when Jesus Christ is revealed to the whole world."[10]

"The boundary lines have fallen for me in pleasant places; surely I have a delightful inheritance."[11]

MERCY AND FORGIVENESS

Sometimes our mission is to bring God's mercy and forgiveness to a merciless and unforgiving world. We might be given an opportunity to exercise the gift of mercy to someone who has deeply wounded us. When we forgive others, we release some of the light of God's Kingdom that will help to drive back the forces of darkness.

Corrie Ten Boom, a Dutch Christian who suffered at the hands of the Nazis during World War II, had a powerful ministry after the war teaching on the power of forgiveness. One day, her tender heart was put to the test when she noticed a gentleman approaching her from the back of the auditorium after she had spoken to a group. To her horror, she immediately recognized him as a guard from the concentration camp where she had been imprisoned.

As the former guard approached, Corrie's mind flashed back to the atrocities she and her sister had suffered at the hands of their captors. She was speechless as the man confessed his crimes and announced that he had come to accept Christ as Savior and had received forgiveness.

"But I would like to hear it from your lips as well," he said.

While he stood waiting for her reply, Corrie remembered the beatings, the inhuman treatment, and the humiliation she had endured in the concentration camp. And she was reminded that her beloved sister, Betsie, had died in that awful place.

But then she remembered how Jesus had willingly gone to the cross to pay all our debts. How he had lovingly forgiven the people who put him there. With a determined act of her will, Corrie chose to forgive this man. Suddenly, the love of Christ flooded her heart, and she embraced the former guard.

"I forgive you, brother, with all my heart!"[12]

Ephesians 4:32 says, "Be kind and compassionate to one another, forgiving each other, just as in Christ God forgave you." Forgiveness is never easy. To wipe away our sins and free us from bondage, it cost Jesus his life. But he paid the price willingly and gladly. In the midst of that kind of grace

. . . how can we hold back forgiveness from others? As we exercise the faith God has given us, and as we step out to *go* as we've been sent, God will move on our behalf.

> Brothers and sisters, think of what you were when you were called. Not many of you were wise by human standards; not many were influential; not many were of noble birth. But God chose the foolish things of the world to shame the wise; God chose the weak things of the world to shame the strong. God chose the lowly things of this world and the despised things—and the things that are not—to nullify the things that are, so that no one may boast before him. It is because of him that you are in Christ Jesus, who has become for us wisdom from God—that is, our righteousness, holiness and redemption. Therefore, as it is written: "Let the one who boasts boast in the Lord."[13]

Close to where I live, God has been doing an amazing work in the town of Gurnee, Illinois. As part of a Go! Project for the Christ Together movement (churches working together within a community), the pastors of ten or so churches decided to team up to reach the local community. In addition to praying together, they decided to share their lists of members with each other. What they discovered was that every area within Gurnee had at least one Christ follower in the neighborhood.[14] This is no coincidence, for when we come to faith in Christ, we become his body, and he strategically places us to share God's love and Kingdom to the world. We are like seeds planted to return a harvest of thirty, sixty, or one hundredfold.[15]

There are very few things we can control in life, but we can direct our own hearts. One of my favorite verses is Proverbs 4:23: "Keep and guard your heart with all vigilance . . . , for out of it flow the springs of life."[16]

To prepare yourself as a fisher of men, walk as closely to Jesus as you can, go boldly to the throne of grace and receive God's mercy, and keep your heart believing and trusting in your Good Shepherd.

AWAKENING TO GOD'S PROVISION: HOW TO BECOME FISHERS OF MEN

[Jesus] said to Simon, "Put out into deep water, and let down the nets for a catch."

Simon answered, "Master, we've worked hard all night and haven't caught anything. But because you say so, I will let down the nets."

When they had done so, they caught such a large number of fish that their nets began to break. So they signaled their partners in the other boat to come and help them, and they came and filled both boats so full that they began to sink.

LUKE 5:4-7

WHEN SIMON (PETER) and his fellow fishermen put out from the shore to go fishing, they took with them all their accumulated knowledge and experience. But they still had no control over whether they would catch any fish. When Jesus came along and told them where to let down their nets, it was despite all their best efforts. In fact, they had been fishing all night without success. But when they followed Jesus' instructions, they soon had more fish than they could handle.

We mustn't forget that before Jesus sent his disciples into the world to make more disciples, he first called them to himself and *showed* them how to do it. "Follow me," he said, "and I will make you fishers of men."[1] In other words, Jesus modeled for us how to walk with God and obey him. Several times Jesus said, "I am here only to do the will of my Father."[2] Obedience to God's will is at the core of being "fishers of men."

With that in mind, here are some principles we can glean from following Christ's example.

DEPEND ON GOD

Jesus said, "I can do nothing on my own. . . . I carry out the will of the one who sent me, not my own will."[3] As in every area of life, when it comes to evangelism, we must depend totally on God.[4] He calls us to be faithful and obedient to his will, but the actual work of salvation is the Holy Spirit's responsibility. Only he can open people's eyes and reveal Jesus to them.[5] When we understand and accept this truth, it removes all the pressure and intensity from our witnessing for Christ.

It doesn't depend on you.

Let that sink in for a moment.

Why then, you might wonder, *are we "fishing for men" in the first place. Why bother?* The answer, in part, is that God allows us and wants us to be a part of his wonderful work of salvation through Jesus Christ. Together, we are Christ's body in the world, and he works in us and through us to reach the lost.

There's no question that God rightly gets all the credit for the salvation of humankind. But there's a pattern and a purpose to how he goes about bringing people to faith in Christ. The great nineteenth-century evangelist D. L. Moody said, "You cannot find . . . a case in the Bible where a man is converted without God's calling in some human agency—using some human instrument."[6]

God has called and equipped you and me to be his ambassadors,[7] and he expects us to be good stewards of the things he has placed in our hands—the relationships, the gifts he has given us, and the opportunities to use those gifts. We steward our hearts by abiding in his love.[8] We steward our time and our gifts by witnessing for Jesus and making new disciples.

We sow and water the seeds, and God causes them to grow and blossom. How the seeds grow and blossom is in God's hands. If we try to control the growth of the seeds, we interfere with God's work. There is no place for pressure, intimidation, control, or fear in God's Kingdom. Instead, God wants us to enjoy walking with him and to experience great joy and peace in joining him in what he is doing to reach lost people through Jesus Christ.

We love to share good news with our friends and family—about a new job, an engagement, or a new baby—so why would we hesitate with the best news we could ever give them? For Christ followers who do not enjoy sharing the gospel with others, it may be they don't understand their role and God's responsibility when it comes to reaching the lost.

Learn to depend on the Holy Spirit in all that you do, especially when it comes to being a "fisher of men." Ask God to give you his heart of compassion for the lost. Ask him for strength and wisdom; more capacity for love, joy, and peace; contacts and opportunities; and all the resources necessary for the work. He is the Lord of the harvest, and he will equip us to carry out his work.[9]

COMMIT YOURSELF TO PRAYER

Ever since Jeannie came to faith in Christ in 1980, she and I have regularly joined together in prayer for our family members. Scripture shows that God can bring whole families into a relationship with him,[10] and we can be bold and confident in praying for God to work in the lives of our family members.[11] Through the years, Jeannie and I have been overjoyed to see her mum, her three brothers, and some of her cousins come to faith in Christ. Also, many of our nephews and nieces have surrendered their lives to Christ, and my eldest brother came back to Christ shortly after my encounter with God in 1980. There are still some family members who are not following Jesus, so we'll continue in our commitment to pray and share as we have opportunity until they all come to faith in Christ.

Jeannie and I have also prayed for our neighbors, and we've seen some of them become Christians as well.

Prayer releases God's Kingdom and his will on earth. Someone has said, "The Lord has given us hands to help the poor, feet to carry the gospel, and knees to go before God in prayer." Of all the tools we've been given to share the gospel, prayer is the most powerful. Consider that you may have only a few brief opportunities to present the message of Christ to others, but you can consistently pray for your friends and family, your neighbors and coworkers, every single day.

To illustrate the power of persistent prayer, Jesus told a parable about a stubborn widow who continually brought her pleas to the lazy local judge. After listening to the widow day after day, the judge was finally so fed up that he granted her request.[12] God is far more compassionate than the unfeeling, annoyed judge in the parable, and he answers our prayers willingly and gladly. Jesus tells us to keep praying for others who need his saving grace and forgiveness. To keep praying for the sister who has lost her way, or the colleague at work who seems so resistant to the gospel. Keep praying, because the Lord hears and answers our pleas.

I'm convinced that someday in heaven, we will meet people who will tell us, "You never knew this, but because you prayed for me every day, I came to faith in Jesus." Keep praying, and watch God work in your life and in the lives of the people around you.

Jeannie and I have long been inspired by the story and example of James and Amelia Taylor, two godly parents who dedicated their infant son, James Hudson Taylor, to the Lord in 1832, praying that God would one day send him as a missionary to China.

As Hudson grew up, he knew nothing of his parents' hopes for his future and instead became a worldly and skeptical young man. But the power of prayer was still working strongly in his life.

One afternoon, Hudson went into his father's study and happened to pick up a gospel tract. Meanwhile, seventy miles away at a friend's house, his mother resolved to plead for her son's salvation until she knew her prayers were answered. That very hour, through the power of persistent prayer, James Hudson Taylor was convicted by the Holy Spirit and surrendered his life to Jesus Christ.

He went on to become perhaps the most influential missionary to China who has ever lived. And prayer continued to be a cornerstone of his ministry. He watched as God answered his requests to change people's hearts, to provide for his physical needs, and to bring more workers onto the mission field. God answered this last prayer specifically in 1885, when he stirred the hearts of seven gifted young men at Cambridge University to commit their lives to join Hudson Taylor in spreading the gospel across China. This group, which included C. T. Studd, became known in missionary circles as the Cambridge Seven, and their sacrifice encouraged thousands of other young people in Great Britain and North America to become missionaries.

Throughout his life, Hudson Taylor had a list of one hundred people he was praying for, and ninety-seven of them came to faith in Christ during his lifetime. The remaining three became Christ followers at his funeral. "The prayer of a righteous person is powerful and effective" indeed![13]

I have run across innumerable examples throughout history of the magnificent power of prayer, as God works through the humble requests of his people. I encourage you to take a minute to think about where you have seen the power of prayer manifested in your own life. Chances are, if you have a relationship with Jesus Christ today, it's because someone prayed for you. Be encouraged and motivated to pray for the salvation of your friends and family.

Start by starting. How should you pray for your family members, neighbors, and coworkers? The best way to learn how to pray is simply to pray! Scripture tells us that the Holy Spirit "helps us in our weakness" and "intercedes for us" as we pray.[14] Start by asking God to fill you with the knowledge of his will, maybe for a particular person or situation.[15] If you've ever felt a special concern for someone, I believe that is the Holy Spirit stirring you to pray for God's Kingdom to come in that person's life.

Ask for God's perspective. Another good prayer is to ask God to give you his compassion for the lost people around you. After you pray this, be sensitive to how the Holy Spirit leads you to pray. Maybe he will wake you up in the night (as he did with the young boy Samuel in the Bible)[16] or put it on your mind to fast for a specific reason. Remember, he wants to use you to bring in his Kingdom; you need only to be available. Stand in faith and believe that the equipping will come along with the calling.

Overcome obstacles. My mind will often tell me that if I get up early to pray, I won't make it through the busy day ahead. But, in reality, I find that the opposite is the case. The more time I spend in God's presence, the stronger and sharper I am throughout the day.

Be persistent. As Winston Churchill famously said, "Never give in. Never, never, never, never."[17] I believe his encouragement and challenge are perfectly applicable to our prayers. God hears our prayers, and in his timing, he will answer. Ask the Lord for grace to accept his answer to your prayer. If your prayer is answered immediately, remember to overflow with thanksgiving to God. If the answer is, "Wait," ask for the patience to persevere. And if the answer is, "No," ask for humility and faith to accept that the Lord has a better plan.

Pray "your kingdom come." When we pray for the Kingdom of God to be seen in our midst, powerful things happen. Our spontaneous cries may be the very tools that God uses to bring heaven down to earth. I have seen remarkable results come from praying according to the example that Jesus gave to his disciples: "Your kingdom come, your will be done, on earth as it is in heaven."[18] Amazingly, our prayers can even change the course of history.

A Christian woman named Monica was having serious problems with her rebellious teenage son. He was lazy, bad-tempered, a liar, and a thief. When he grew up to be a successful lawyer, his life was consumed by selfish ambition and greed. His morals were loose, and he adopted all kinds of strange religious practices.

Throughout this time, his mother kept praying "your kingdom come" prayers for his life. One day, she had a vision that the light of Jesus Christ was shining on her son's face, and this encouraged her to pray all the more. Still, nine more years passed before her son finally gave his life to Christ at the age of thirty-two.

That young man's name was Augustine—now known by many as *Saint* Augustine. He was converted in AD 386, ordained in 391, and became a bishop in 396. Today, he is remembered as perhaps the greatest theologian of the church. Augustine always attributed his conversion to the faithful prayers of his mother.

This story gives us great hope that no person or situation is too difficult for God. In our own lives, we want our family members, neighbors, and coworkers to come to faith in Christ, but there will probably be several steps along the way. Therefore, you may be led to pray strategically in the following ways:

- That God will send other Christians to be additional links in the process—perhaps a new friend or coworker who is also a Christ follower.[19]
- That the people for whom you're praying will see the wonders of creation and begin to consider the reality of God.[20]
- That they will consider, and be concerned about, the afterlife (maybe after the death of a friend or family member).
- That God will open the eyes of their hearts to his love through a felt need in their family (e.g., marital problems or challenges with children).

- That God will give you an opportunity to show them his kindness.[21]

God wants to use you to accomplish his will here on earth. I encourage you to stop and think about the people for whom you are praying today. If there are no names on that list, spend some time in prayer asking the Lord to direct your prayers for a specific person or group of people. Why not start a "ten most wanted" list of family, friends, neighbors, and coworkers—a special group you will pray for, from here on, every day.

CONCENTRATE ON *BEING* RATHER THAN DOING

To be effective as fishers of men, it's important that we spend time with people outside the church. Jesus showed us how to do this. He came and lived among us—or, as Eugene Peterson puts it in *The Message*, "The Word became flesh and blood, and moved into the neighborhood."[22] For the first thirty years of his life, Jesus simply lived, worked, and played with the people who were around him. Even after he was anointed by the Holy Spirit for public ministry, he still lived and walked among the common people. He ate and partied with all types of people, the outcasts and the well-to-do. He was with people in the world, and he prayed that his followers would remain in the world but be kept safe from the evil one.[23]

D. L. Moody once said, "Christians should live in the world, but not be filled with it. A ship lives in the water; but if the water gets into the ship, she goes to the bottom. So Christians may live in the world; but if the world gets into them, they sink."[24] It is the very thing the apostle James has in mind when he writes, "Keep . . . from being polluted by the world."[25]

When Christians don't *go* into the world as salt and light, the forces of darkness are able to take over the spiritual realm. Unfortunately, the prevailing Western model of church is different from what Jesus told us to do. We tend to follow a *"come"* model that focuses on getting people to come to church to hear the gospel. But Jesus told us to *go* and make disciples out in the world where the people already are. When we *go* into the world, people will *come* into the church.

Sadly, for many Christians, it seems their first impulse when they come to faith in Christ is to distance themselves from their old identities—and from the people with whom they associated. And though our awakened hearts will quite naturally begin to change, and those changes will radiate throughout our thoughts, words, and actions, there's something to be said for not forgetting where we've been—the mud and mire from which we've been lifted. For it's in remembering our desperate state that we find our motivation to see others lifted up as well.

Returning to a *go* model of evangelism means making friends with "lost people" and making it a priority to spend time with them.[26] God wants you to be his hands and feet, his ears and mouth—to hear people's views, to feel their pain, to share their joy, and to give them the good news of life with Jesus. Your job is not to bring judgment, but rather to love people and to show them what the Kingdom of God looks like.

To rest and relax, I enjoy playing golf on Saturday mornings with some of my good friends, and we always try to include in our foursome at least one person who doesn't know Christ. One year, a retired Navy SEAL joined our group. He was a great guy, built like a tank, but on the first Saturday we quickly learned that his vocabulary was anchored soundly in profanity. No one said anything to him about it, and for the next several Saturdays, the air around this man turned blue every time he opened his mouth. But a few weeks in, we began to notice a decrease in the amount of swearing from him, and over the course of the summer he swore less and less, until we hardly heard any profanity at all during our rounds.

My friends and I talked naturally about the Lord while we played, but I don't think any of us directly shared the gospel with our new friend. At the end of the season, he wrote to thank us for the fun he'd had playing golf with us, and then he wrote, "I want you to know that every time I joined you guys on Saturday morning, I felt an energy and a joy coming out of you. It inspired and encouraged me, and I always felt uplifted by the end of the round." He later accepted an invitation to come to an Alpha introductory dinner, though I don't know what happened to him after that.

Remembering Christ's example of spending time with people who need to hear the gospel, I look for opportunities to make friends with people who don't know Christ. Sometimes I make specific plans to do this, and other times it is simply part of the normal rhythm of life.

BUILD RELATIONSHIPS ON TRUST

In loving the people around us, we need to "build bridges of trust that are strong enough to bear the truth."[27] As we build genuine friendships with people, we allow them to see and experience something of the Kingdom of God in us. Developing trust opens up opportunities to share about Jesus Christ. Where I live in Chicago, the ground is typically frozen for six months of the year. If we were to sow seeds during those months, we'd be wasting our time. Nothing will take. However, if we sow when the earth is soft and well-watered, the seeds will take and we'll eventually enjoy a harvest. We must first allow God's love and presence within us to soften the hearts of our friends; then, as led by the Holy Spirit, we can share about Jesus.

Years ago, when I was working at the bank, I remember waiting for about a year before I felt I had a real opening to speak to my colleagues about Jesus. The pressure in our office was intense, with a lot of young, ambitious people looking to advance their careers, and it took a while to establish open, trusting relationships. Then, one day, while we were all sitting around chatting, someone asked me about my faith. It was as if the presence of God came upon me at that moment. I was able to share, in front of everybody, my love for Jesus and my desire to serve him. After that, several of my coworkers wanted to hear more about Christ. This experience taught me that sometimes you have to wait until the time is right to put words to the seeds that are being sown through your actions and attitude.

PARTNER WITH OTHER BELIEVERS

I've made it a point to show that Jesus clearly called us to *go*, but it's important to note that he called us to go in a specific way: *with at least one other person.*[28] As soon as we go into the world to make disciples for Jesus, we begin to push back the darkness of the enemy, and we engage in the cosmic battle taking place for the souls of men and women. Partnering with another person adds strength to the mission. As the wise King Solomon writes, "Though one may be overpowered, two can defend themselves. A cord of three strands is not quickly broken."[29] Partnering is especially important in times of disappointment and discouragement.[30]

When Jeannie and I lived in London, we often reached out to the people living or working nearby. Sometimes, we went door-to-door with surveys and other initiatives, but we always went in pairs. When I started to become more intentional about reaching out in my workplace, it began with prayer with a close friend of mine. He and I were often discouraged by people's responses—and, sometimes, their aggressive reactions. But, somehow, being with a friend enabled us to encourage one another and to continue with the work.

In my travels across America, many pastors have shared

with me that the people in their congregations have been disheartened with the various evangelistic initiatives they've tried. Maybe you feel the same way. You tried to witness for Christ, but nothing seemed to work, and eventually you gave up. Now when your pastor, priest, or someone else mentions a new evangelistic initiative, you have a sinking feeling in your heart, and your mind automatically begins to make excuses: *This program isn't relevant for me. I don't have the gift of evangelism.*

I encourage you to start afresh today. The call to *go* is for every Christ follower. But if you find someone to *go with*, I believe it will dramatically change the experience for you.

If you are married, your spouse is an obvious person to go with. But, you could also go with someone else.

When I worked for HSBC in the City of London, my friend and colleague Mike Campbell and I believed that God had planted us in the bank "for such a time as this."[31] We believed he wanted to use us to bless people in our work environment and thereby bring in a bit of God's Kingdom. So, Mike and I agreed to arrive at work one day per week about thirty minutes early, and we started praying together for our work, our witness, and our coworkers. We prayed for God's Kingdom to come and his will to be done in the bank.[32] We prayed for each other that God would fill us with his Holy Spirit and grant us his grace and power to be strong and courageous to glorify him in our workplace. And we prayed, as Jesus had instructed his disciples, that the Father would send more laborers to help us in the harvest field in which he had planted us.[33] It was a very simple approach, but because it was in line with God's will to reach people with the gospel, we saw amazing answers.[34]

Keep in mind that we were right in the middle of the City of London—the financial center of Europe (and, arguably, of the world). This was Satan's stronghold, where the love of money ruled supreme. At first glance, it was an environment obsessed with financial gain and growth, not a place where you'd expect to find many active Christians. However, as we committed ourselves to prayer, we started bumping into other Christ followers who expressed an interest in joining our daily time of prayer and outreach. Encouraged by this, as well as by the discovery of other Christian HSBC employees who were praying in the Sheffield office and in other parts of the bank, we obtained permission to place a notice in the staff bulletin, inviting others at the bank to join us. Within a few weeks, more than one hundred Christ followers had signed up, and we had six prayer groups meeting in bank buildings across London. When the executive management group heard what was going on, some of them spoke at our meetings and encouraged us in what we were doing. A number of people came to faith in Christ during this time, and the Kingdom of God started to break out in the City of London. When Mike and I decided to obey God's Word to pray and reach out together for God's Kingdom to come where we were planted, we had no idea we would be joining in on a work that God already had underway in our city.

LOOK FOR SOMEONE WHO PROMOTES PEACE

The Bible contains some wonderful "nuggets of gold," and one in particular that pertains to our mission of being fishers of men is the principle of seeking a person of peace wherever we go.[35]

> The Lord appointed seventy-two others and sent them two by two ahead of him to every town and place where he was about to go. He told them, "The harvest is plentiful, but the workers are few. Ask the Lord of the harvest, therefore, to send out workers into his harvest field. Go! I am sending you out like lambs among wolves. Do not take a purse or bag or sandals; and do not greet anyone on the road.
>
> "When you enter a house, first say, 'Peace to this house.' If someone who promotes peace is there, your peace will rest on them; if not, it will return to you."[36]

At one point in his earthly ministry, Jesus sent out teams of disciples to the towns where he intended to go, to prepare the way for his coming. Because we have the same mission today—preparing the way for the coming of the Lord—we can learn several key principles from this example.

First, as we've already noted, Jesus sent the disciples out in pairs. Next, he told them to *pray* that God would send even more workers out into the "harvest." (If you're still sitting on the sidelines, this nudge is for you.) He told them to *go*, even though they may have felt unprepared—like lambs among wolves, and without any baggage—and not to be called aside from the task by any distractions, or stretched too thin by trying to reach too many at once.

Finally, he told them to carry the peace of God with them, and to offer that peace to those they encountered. When they found "someone who promotes peace," that was where they were to invest their efforts. Whatever else we might glean from this passage, I believe it instructs us not to be confrontational or anxious in our approach to people, but to go forward with the settled peace of God resting upon us.

We can spend vast amounts of precious time and energy "fishing" in the wrong place and at the wrong time. When I lived in central London, we often prayed that God would deliver us from *time wasters*. With thousands of needy people all around us, we really needed to discern where God wanted us to focus our attention. Who were the people he wanted us to spend our time and resources on? Who exactly were the persons of peace?

A person of peace is someone who shows interest in the Kingdom of God. That is, there is some indication that the Holy Spirit has already been working in the person's life to draw him or her to Jesus. Because the Kingdom of God is, first of all, of the Spirit, one way to recognize a person of peace is that he or she will have an interest in spiritual things.

Don't be put off by people who say they're interested in meditation or New Age. It shows they're searching. Deep inside, they want more! One of the most powerful conversions I have ever witnessed was of a middle-aged woman who had tried all sorts of different religions and spiritual activity. When she finally encountered Jesus during an Alpha course, she knew she had met the one her soul had been searching for, and she wept deeply as God's love filled her heart through the Holy Spirit. She later became a great fisher of men.

In the workplace, the neighborhood, or the town square, it's great fun to "fish" for the person of peace. I do this by sharing something of the Kingdom of God in my everyday conversation. For example, the conversation might go something like this:

"Hi, Mike, you're looking very relaxed this morning. How was your weekend?"

"I had a great weekend, Gerard. Managed to rest a bit on Saturday and then had a great game of soccer on Sunday morning, followed by a barbecue and a few beers with some friends. How about you?"

"Yeah, we had a great weekend too. Time with the family, including a movie on Saturday. A fantastic time at church on Sunday morning, and then did some work in the garden in the afternoon."

If Mike is a person of peace—that is, if the Holy Spirit has been preparing his heart to receive the Good News—he may well come back to me regarding my mention of having a fantastic time at church. Or it could be someone who overhears our conversation. If there's an interest in spiritual things, that person might say something like, "Gerard, did I

hear you say you had a great time at church? My experience
of church has always been boring and miserable, but never
'fantastic.'"

When I get a probing response to a spiritual topic, I
believe I have found a person of peace. That doesn't mean I'll
jump straight in with the gospel, but I take it as a prompting
from the Holy Spirit to "stay there" and to begin intentionally looking for opportunities to develop a relationship. In
fact, it might be several months before I actually share the
gospel or invite the person to Alpha.

The key is to be absolutely natural and honest. Don't
fabricate, because people will see straight through it. People
today are desperate for authenticity. Be sensitive to where
they are on their journey. Speak the truth in love. Be honest
about what God has done, and is doing, in your life.

Prayer is often a subject that a person of peace will respond
to. If someone received healing after prayer, or if you're praying for a difficult situation with your children, mention it
in your conversations with people outside of the church.
However, it must be natural. There is no need to change the
tone of your voice or make it sound super-spiritual—that
might only make people think you're odd. You want people
to see that the Kingdom of God is very real, very practical,
and very near!

Sometimes I'll ask if I can pray for a person or a situation
that someone has mentioned to me or of which I'm aware.
If I feel it's appropriate—based on the circumstance, the setting, and the level of relationship—I may ask if I can pray

with the person there and then. Obviously, you don't want to embarrass anyone, so be careful about how and when you ask this question.

While working for the bank, I got into a conversation early one morning with a janitor. He mentioned he was worried about his wife, who was very sick back home in Africa. There were a few other people in the office at the time, but I sensed I should offer to pray with the man for his wife to get better. To avoid embarrassment, we went into another room. Later that week, he was delighted to tell me that his wife had started to get better right around the time we prayed.

There are many other ways to find persons of peace among the people God has placed around us. For example, I used to have a calendar on my desk with Scripture verses on it, and someone asked me about it one time, which led to further conversation. I developed a rather keen ear in conversations for any sign of spiritual interest (which, again, was not necessarily my cue to immediately introduce the gospel, but which opened my eyes to possible persons of peace), and I would occasionally invite others to events in and out of the church where they might be exposed to the gospel. The principle is to throw some groundbait on the water to attract the fish, and then to have our spiritual antennae up to recognize a response.[37]

It's important to remember that the person of peace may not be one and the same with the person immediately before us. I heard of one pastor who got into a conversation with a bartender, and she asked him what he did for work. When he said he was a pastor, she said, "That's great. My grandfather has become very interested in the Bible and keeps asking me all these questions. I have no idea what he's talking about, but would you mind if I invited him to meet you?" Of course the pastor agreed, and he met the girl's grandfather. They struck up a friendship, and the man later came to faith in Christ.

SHOW PEOPLE THE KINGDOM OF GOD

God wants us to show people what his love looks like. This of course includes authentic friendships. When we show a genuine interest in people, their family situations, their likes and dislikes, their challenges, and the areas in which they need prayer, we create opportunities to show them God's love. Building friendships takes time—and it's part of our central *mission* and *purpose* in life, not merely an evangelistic technique. Jesus was called "a friend of sinners,"[38] which meant he was willing to meet people where they were in life and to genuinely care about them. By developing friendships and building trust, he showed people what the Kingdom of God looks like. What it is and what it isn't.

In your friendships, you can show people that the Kingdom of God is not about rules and regulations, but rather about living an abundant life of love, joy, and peace. You can let people see and experience the love in your marriage and in your other relationships. And you can look for ways to bless them[39] and to pray for them to be healed.[40] Also, as people observe your life, they will see that the Kingdom of God is very different from the world they are living in. It doesn't include immorality, backbiting, crude jokes, getting drunk, taking drugs, cheating, or tax avoidance. You don't necessarily have to tell your friends these things; they will see it in how you live.

KEEP YOUR HEART FREE FROM DISCOURAGEMENT AND DISAPPOINTMENT

When things don't work out the way we hoped or planned, it's very natural to feel discouraged and disappointed. I find that being a fisher of men can be very encouraging at times, but also extremely discouraging at other times. When we pour into people's lives, they can seem so close to coming to faith in Christ, and it's hard not to be disappointed if they turn away at the last moment. It's also easy to feel discouraged when someone makes a confession of faith but then falls back into a life of sin and selfishness.

Behind these feelings is a voice that says, "God is not in control." It's a voice of unbelief, and if we don't brush it off, it can undermine our faith. If we believe the lie that God is not in control of the past, present, and future, it will hinder our trust in him.

The best way to deal with discouragement and disappointment is through prayer—direct to the Father. Tell him how you feel and ask him to fill you afresh with the Holy Spirit and to cleanse your conscience and wash you of any misplaced guilt or fear. Remember, as you *go*, God has promised to be with you and to equip you to do his will.

Now may the God of peace, who through the blood of the eternal covenant brought back from the dead our Lord Jesus, that great Shepherd of the sheep, equip you with everything good for doing his will, and may he work in us what is pleasing to him, through Jesus Christ, to whom be glory for ever and ever. Amen.[41]

8

AWAKENING TO THE NETS:
HOW TO DRAW IN THE FISH

*Go quickly into the great streets and the small streets of the city
and bring in here the poor and the disabled and the blind and the
lame. . . . Go out into the highways and hedges and urge and constrain
[them] to yield and come in, so that my house may be filled.*

LUKE 14:21, 23, AMP

IF WE REALLY love people, our ultimate concern will be their eternal destiny. Every second of every day, three people pass from this age into eternity, either into heaven or into hell. We must be as earnest and wholehearted as the apostle Paul was when he urged the Corinthians "not to receive God's grace in vain. For [God] says, 'In the time of my favor I heard you, and in the day of salvation I helped you.' I tell you, *now* is the time of God's favor, *now* is the day of salvation."[1] As Christ's ambassadors, our job is to show people what the Kingdom of God is like and to invite them to receive God's gift of salvation through Jesus Christ.[2] And may we "put no stumbling block in anyone's path, so that our ministry will not be discredited."[3]

It's one thing not to place a stumbling block in someone's way, but how can we actually *draw* people toward placing their faith in Jesus Christ? In this chapter, we're going to consider the things that will soften people's hearts and bring them closer to God. Here are some ways in which you can model God's love to your friends, relatives, and acquaintances who don't yet know Christ.

LOVE ONE ANOTHER

As a follower of Jesus, your witness is directly linked to your commitment and care for other people. "By this everyone will know that you are my disciples, if you love one another."[4] When you love people, especially in the midst of danger or trials, it's a powerful reflection of God's sacrificial love.

In the late 1800s, Father Damien, a Roman Catholic priest from Belgium, modeled Jesus' love and kindness in a remarkable way. While serving on the "Big Island" of Hawaii, he felt called to minister to a quarantined colony of lepers on the island of Molokai. There he built a church, enlarged the hospital, and cared for the physical and medical needs of the sick. In a letter to his brother, Damien wrote, "I make myself a leper with the lepers to gain all to Jesus Christ."

Fifteen years later, Father Damien himself contracted leprosy and gave his life in the service of those he loved. Through his sacrificial actions, he demonstrated the power of Jesus' love by becoming a servant to the lowly and the broken.

BE PATIENT

I'm increasingly amazed by God's patience with me. So many times I've messed up and let him down, and yet he never gives up on me! By God's grace, we can and should show the same patience with our family and friends, for "love is patient."[5]

Jeannie and I have several friends whom we've been reaching out to for more than thirty years, and we're still waiting and praying for them to come to faith in Christ. In these times, we hold tight to God's plan, knowing, "Love never gives up, never loses faith, is always hopeful, and endures through every circumstance."[6]

DEMONSTRATE KINDNESS

I have observed that kindness is one of the most powerful ways to reach people with the love of God. In what seems to be an increasingly selfish world, acts of kindness and selflessness stand out as shining lights in the darkness.

Even simple acts of kindness can have a profound impact.

Years ago, while on a residential training course with some of my colleagues from the bank, I noticed that one of my friends had failed to turn up for the evening meal. I often miss opportunities like this, but I felt a particular prompting by the Holy Spirit to check up on my friend. I excused myself from the dinner table and went up to John's room. Knocking on his door, I gently said, "John, I noticed you weren't at dinner this evening, and I just wanted to check if you're okay and to see if I can do anything for you." John thanked me for asking and said he was feeling unwell and just wanted an early night.

A short time later, John came to faith in Christ, and he said that my simple act of kindness had been the "tipping point" for his conversion.

Another example of how kindness releases the Kingdom of God occurred in the central London church I was serving in. The congregation there did a fantastic job of caring for the local people. One person who was deeply affected was Husain, a Muslim from North Africa. When Husain and his wife and children moved to London as refugees, they desperately needed help. Some members of the church took Husain and his family under their wing and helped to establish them with a home, clothing, furniture, and food. Husain and his family were deeply touched by the kindness shown to them, and they later came to faith in Christ.

RESPECT PEOPLE BY HOW YOU LISTEN

Every human being is made in the image of God and is highly valued by him. God loves the whole world so much that he sent Jesus to die on behalf of every soul on the planet. God has no favorites. Everyone has equal value in his eyes. If anyone has been blessed with gifts such as great wisdom, wealth, beauty, strength, or sporting ability, it's only because God has given these gifts to them.[7] However, in God's economy, a person who appears to have few or no gifts has the same value as someone more obviously gifted.

A great way to introduce people to God's love is by

showing them respect and genuinely listening to what they say. Although you may not agree with other people's views and opinions, you can still respect them, recognizing that we're all at different points in our journeys through life. I encourage you to develop your listening skills—look people in the eye, use nonverbal communication to show that they have your attention (nodding, sitting forward, maintaining open posture), repeat what they say to show that you've heard, and thank them for sharing their thoughts and views. If you're someplace where it's hard to talk, maybe suggest meeting up for a coffee and a chat at a later time.

Many people think that God can't possibly be interested in them. You can help to show God's compassion for them by how you listen to and respect their views.

DO NOT JUDGE

It's not your place to convict people of their sin; that's the Holy Spirit's job.[8] If you judge people, you interfere with what God is doing to bring them to Christ. Often, it creates a wall of pride that prevents people from hearing the gospel. Your job is simply to love people the way God loves you.

I've heard many stories of people whose lifestyles are out of step with the Kingdom of God but who felt loved and accepted (and not judged) when they attended an Alpha course. That's how it should be in *all* their encounters with followers of Christ. In an environment of love and acceptance, people are able to hear the truth of the gospel and come to faith in Jesus Christ. In God's love, there is light and power. Through the Holy Spirit, God's light shines into their hearts, convicting them of their sin and giving them the power to repent, turn around, and go God's way.[9]

By intentionally accepting people right where they are on their journeys, in a broken and messed up world, you can create an environment in which their hearts can be softened so they can hear and receive the seed of the gospel.

I have seen firsthand how an environment of love and acceptance has helped hundreds of people come to faith in Christ. The following story illustrates the importance of making sure we never judge people—and also how powerful it is when we obey the promptings of the Holy Spirit.

Julie is a great "fisher of men" who is attuned to the Holy Spirit's leading. One day, she sensed the Holy Spirit telling her that she was going to meet someone whom she should invite to the Alpha course at my home in central London. Sure enough, later that day she got into a conversation with a guy named Bill. Julie didn't know this, but Bill had had a dream two nights before that God was going to do something in his life.

Bill didn't know Christ, and his life was a mess—he was a drug addict and a gang member, had children from multiple relationships, had been depressed for seven years, and hadn't worked for five of those years. As you might imagine, he was an angry man. He was also tall and intimidating. Therefore, when he turned up at our door to attend Alpha, I had a mind to tell him he'd come to the wrong house!

Although he was very aggressive and antagonistic

throughout the evening (especially during the group discussion time), he came back time and again. It was a great course with several guys who didn't know Christ, including another drug addict and an atheist.

As far as I know, none of these men came to faith in Christ during that first course, but they all asked if they could do the course again. In their second Alpha course, it was clear that God's love and Kingdom was breaking into their lives.

After one of the evenings, I invited Bill to come to church. I was overjoyed when he walked into church the next Sunday and even more excited when he came forward for prayer at the end of the service. As we gently laid our hands on Bill, the Holy Spirit started to pour God's love into his heart. He began to weep like a baby as he met the God who so desperately loves him. There was a pool of tears where he was standing, and he received Jesus as his Savior that Sunday.

The next morning when he woke up, he was totally healed of his depression, and the day after that he got a job as a sales rep. By the following week, he was promoted to manager of the sales team; such was the complete transformation that had taken place in his life through the power of the gospel of Jesus Christ.

As wonderful as this story is, I want you to particularly hear this next point. I asked Bill why he had returned week after week to Alpha, even though it was obvious his lifestyle was completely different from ours. Here's what Bill said to me: "I came back because you never judged me."

If you judge people, they won't stick around. (Who likes

feeling judged?) If they don't stick around, they won't hear the gospel, and they may miss the opportunity to come to faith in Christ, to receive eternal life, and to be with us in heaven forever.

SHOW MERCY AND GRACE

Thank God that he doesn't deal with you and me as we deserve! Instead, because of Jesus' sacrifice on the cross, God's mercy triumphs over judgment.[10] If this is how God forgives us and shows his mercy to us, then we should forgive and show mercy to other people.[11] In showing mercy, we reveal to people what the Kingdom of God is like.

Through God's grace, we receive what we don't deserve. One of the privileges I've had in leading more than fifty Alpha courses is seeing the grace of God touch people's lives in a remarkable way. Sometimes, we think conversion can only happen when we follow a rigid sequence of events. However, it rarely happens like that, and only God knows when someone is properly "born again."[12] I have seen many people touched by the Holy Spirit with healing, joy, and great love before they ever said the sinner's prayer.

One thing we know is that God desperately loves every person in the world, and he is in the rescue business. And he often chooses to reach the most unlikely candidates.

John Newton, who lived during the eighteenth century, was a militant atheist, bully, and blasphemer. People described him as a wild and angry young man. At the age of eighteen, he was forced to join the navy. There, he recklessly

broke the rules and was eventually publicly flogged for deser-
tion. He was hated and feared by his crewmates, and after his
time in the navy, he went on to become a slave trader.

At the age of twenty-three, Newton's slave ship encountered a severe storm off the coast of Ireland and almost sank.
Fearing for his life, he called out to God. And on that day,
March 10, 1748, God rescued him. Newton's life was spared,
and he began to explore the Christian faith.

In time, John Newton became an Anglican minister and
influenced leaders such as William Wilberforce. But it's possible he's best known today for his enduring hymn: "Amazing
grace! How sweet the sound that saved a wretch like me."

God's mercy and grace are so beautiful and so attractive.
You can bring people closer to placing their faith in Jesus
Christ by showing them what God's mercy and grace look
like.

FORGIVE

Saul of Tarsus was not someone you would expect God to
use to spread the gospel around the Middle East and to
write much of the New Testament. He was a devout Jewish
Pharisee, intent on keeping every letter of the law. He was
also set on stamping out anyone who veered from this path,
including and most especially a growing sect who called
themselves Christians. In fact, Saul went on several journeys
to see about putting these religious fanatics to death. But
along the way one day, Saul came face-to-face with the very
person he was fighting against: Jesus Christ.

After Saul's dramatic conversion, which included changing his name to Paul, he went on to become perhaps the greatest evangelist and theologian the church has ever known. Paul traveled extensively, sharing the Good News. His passion for Jesus was unchecked. Even beatings, imprisonment, stonings, shipwrecks, and slanderous remarks couldn't discourage him from his mission. Once he had put others to death for their belief in Jesus, but ultimately Paul himself was martyred for aligning himself unapologetically with Jesus Christ.

If God can forgive and transform someone like Paul, he can do the same for *any* of the people you know. No one is beyond God's love and transforming power. Also, maybe God will challenge you to show forgiveness to a family member or a friend and, in that way, show them a key part of the Kingdom of God.

BE EXTRAVAGANTLY GENEROUS

God's grace, mercy, and forgiveness reveal to us his extravagant generosity. He has given us everything we need for abundant eternal life.[13] We are destined for blessing, even in our trials and tribulations.[14] The longer we go on with Christ, the more we realize how true this is.

When we see how blessed we are and that everything we have is a gift from God to share with other people, we will want to emulate God's extravagant generosity. Go over the top in blessing people in any way you can, and watch the Kingdom of God start to break out in their lives.

Jesus said, "I have come that they may have life, and that

they may have it more abundantly."[15] It's important for people outside the church to know that they can live lives of peace and contentment in God's Kingdom without having to resort to immorality, drugs, alcoholism, cheating, lying, and the like.

When I was pastoring in London, we used to make our home group a party for people outside the church on every fourth Thursday of the month. The purpose was not to try to convert people, but to bless them and have lots of fun.

Satan has worked hard to make people think that if they become Christians, they will be miserable, when, in fact, the opposite is often the case. Christ followers should have the best marriages and the happiest families, be the most content in their jobs, and be genuine, authentic, honest people who are willing to say, "I've had a bad day," but also to model God's peace at the same time. As we live our lives with a God-given abundance of love, joy, peace, patience, kindness, goodness, faithfulness, gentleness, and self-control,[16] people outside of the church will naturally notice these values and gifts of the Kingdom of God and be drawn to Christ. It's interesting that when Jesus sent his disciples out, he sent them to the people he was about to visit.[17] Our role in the Kingdom is to help prepare the hearts of people to receive Jesus.

USE THE SPECIAL GIFTS THAT GOD HAS PLACED IN YOUR HANDS

God has an amazing way of taking the most painful areas of our lives and making something beautiful out of them. For Jeannie and me, God has entrusted us with the gift of brokenness. Not a day goes by that we don't think about and miss our son Alex. But through our pain, God has touched many people and brought them into his eternal Kingdom. I know of at least two work colleagues who came to faith in Christ shortly after Alex's death.

One of them was a guy named Ed, who worked with me at the bank. He was an agnostic and used to gently poke fun at my faith in Christ. After Alex died, Ed began to watch me closely, and he came to Alex's memorial service. At the service, he heard the gospel and saw many people stand up to receive Christ. God touched Ed during the service, as well, and he came away thinking, *I've got to find out if this is true.* He decided to attend the next Alpha course we had and came to faith in Christ.

Sadly, during the course, Ed discovered he had cancer. His dear wife, Pattie, became very confused because, despite the worrying diagnosis, Ed had tremendous peace through his faith in Jesus. Pattie decided to find out why Ed had such peace, and she also came to faith in Christ after attending the next Alpha course. Ed and Pattie became great small group leaders and served until Ed went to be with the Lord a few years later. Pattie remains a good friend of ours.

Over the years, we have been able to empathize with and come alongside many parents who have lost children to suicide. And our daughter, Rebecca, often writes to the siblings.

What gift has God placed in your hands that he wants you to use—at the right time and in the right way—to help and reach others? Maybe you've been through a broken relationship or a failed business; health struggles or financial ruin; or maybe God has delivered you from an addiction. Nothing is ever wasted in the Kingdom of God,[18] and if you will let him, God will use you to comfort and reach other people who are experiencing something similar to what you have been through.[19]

HIGHLIGHT THE VALUES OF THE KINGDOM OF GOD

I look for opportunities to let people know they are not far from the Kingdom of God. If I see or hear about a great act of service, extravagant generosity, or a wonderful example of kindness, I will say something like, "I hope you don't mind me saying so, but what you just did was a very special act of kindness to that person. And I don't know if you know this, but you showed something of God's heart and love by what you just did, and I know he is pleased by your action." In saying this, I send many messages to the recipient: God is a person; God wants to encourage you and lift you up; you're not as far from God as you may think; and God is good, and he does good things.

I look for special events in people's lives to encourage them to consider that maybe God is behind the good thing that has just happened to them. I remember an agnostic friend of mine recalling the wonder of his newborn child. He told me, "When we had our baby, I was struck by her beauty and was amazed by the whole thing. And I went outside and I looked up and said, 'I don't know if you're up there, but if you are, I just want to say, "Thank you."'"

Even those who don't have a personal relationship with Jesus recognize the wonder of his goodness. And even those who don't know God still reflect his image when they show kindness, generosity, and love to others.

Your job as a follower of Jesus is to help people see those traces of good in their lives and to point them to the giver of "every good and perfect gift."[20] As you take time to look, you will see evidence of God's presence and power all around you.

DEMONSTRATE THAT YOUR LIFE IS IN CHRIST AND NOT IN YOUR POSSESSIONS

When Jeannie and I first moved to London, we lived below the poverty line and survived on gifts from friends. When we were eventually able to purchase our first house, we could afford only minimal decorations—it was all very plain. However, we had tremendous contentment through Jesus Christ, and two of our "materialistic" friends came to faith in Christ because they saw we had a source of life that didn't depend on our possessions. In our wealth-obsessed culture, the peace, contentment, and joy we have in Christ, regardless of our circumstances, will draw people toward the God who loves them and desires to bless them.

9

AWAKENING TO THE CATCH: HOW TO LAND THE FISH

But how shall they ask him to save them unless they believe in him?
And how can they believe in him if they have never heard about
him? And how can they hear about him unless someone tells them?
ROMANS 10:14, TLB

Always be ready to give a logical defense to anyone
who asks you to account for the hope that is in
you, but do it courteously and respectfully.
I PETER 3:15, AMP

You've *GONE*. You've *fished*. And now—quite suddenly, it seems—you've got a live one on the line.

Now what?

As any fisherman will tell you, a fish isn't *caught* until it's safely in the boat. If we're not careful at the point of transition, it's possible to lose a fish at the very last moment. As it pertains to "fishing for people," we must remain sensitive to the promptings of the Holy Spirit as to when to encourage a person to repent and receive Jesus as Lord and Savior.

Here are some ways I've learned to gently and carefully "bring someone aboard."

ASK QUESTIONS

In the Gospels, Jesus is asked 278 questions. He answers only three of them, but he asks 307 questions of his own. Have you ever noticed that you have a much better grasp of information when you've had to think it through for yourself? I suspect that's why Jesus was much more apt to ask a question than to answer one.

Sometimes, as Christians, we avoid discussing our faith in Jesus with people outside the church because we think we have to know all the answers to any questions they might raise. But that's not true. I encourage you to think about "witnessing" in a different way. Start by sharing what your relationship with Jesus means to you, and then ask questions. For example, "Do you believe there is a God? If so, what is he like? Do you believe there is a heaven and a hell?" Encouraging people to think more deeply about spiritual things will prepare the way for them to come to faith in Christ.

I've come to the view that it's best to encourage people to consider the person of Jesus rather than getting into debates about theological issues, such as creationism versus evolution. However, you may want to encourage people to question their beliefs on evolution and to consider the evidence for God in the incredible beauty we see in creation. One of my colleagues at the bank came to faith in Christ after first reconsidering genetics and evolution. Personally, I find it much simpler and more feasible to believe the scriptural account of creation. "By faith we understand that the worlds [during the successive ages] were framed (fashioned, put in order, and equipped for their intended purpose) by the word of God, so that what we see was not made out of things which are visible."[1]

USE VARIOUS MEDIA

As you develop relationships with people outside of the church, there will come a time when you can ask them to consider the person of Jesus Christ. But in the meantime, there are many ways to encourage and feed their interest or curiosity about the Christian faith, including sending them clips of *The Bible* television series or the *JESUS* film (both of which are available as smartphone apps),[2] or inviting them to watch the movie *Son of God* with you and asking for their thoughts and views afterward. Remember, asking questions is often more profitable than making statements.

You might also send them a Christian book to match where you think they are on their journey. If they're just beginning, perhaps send a testimony to get them to consider Christ. If they are further along on their faith journey, maybe give them a copy of C. S. Lewis's *Mere Christianity* or Nicky Gumbel's *Questions of Life*.

A few years back, I heard about a remarkable lady named Bonnie Lee Colquhoun, who had been a Christ follower all of her life. Her strong faith had helped her survive an early, abusive marriage, including the loss of an unborn child (after she was thrown down a flight of stairs). Bonnie's gentle strength, combined with her faith, enabled her to raise three children who all accepted Christ by the time they were adults.

After a lifetime of Bible study and church attendance, Bonnie had a life-defining experience in her mideighties, when she signed up for an Alpha course. "It reinforced her faith," says her son, Jeff. "It also shaped her understanding of biblical doctrine and helped prepare her for what was ahead."

Two years later, Bonnie was diagnosed with ovarian cancer, and the prognosis wasn't good. Though an avid reader, she eventually became too sick even to read, so Jeff began reading aloud to her to keep her mind alert and to provide a diversion from her suffering. One of the first books he picked up was *The Breakthrough*, a parable I had written to encourage people to consider the following questions: Is there more to life than what I'm seeing? Is there a heaven and a hell? Is how I'm living my life hurting other people?[3]

"As soon as we got into the book," Jeff says, "she was captivated. She loved the story of David Heeley, especially how he came to Christ, and how faith can transform a family. I'm so glad I was able to share *The Breakthrough* with my mom. It gave her purpose in her final days, and hearing the story shifted her focus from suffering to hope in Christ."

Bonnie was so taken with *The Breakthrough* and its implications for sharing the gospel that she asked Jeff to order twelve copies. "They didn't last long," he says. "Mom began giving them to people who visited her in hospice, the hospice staff, and anyone else she came in contact with. She spent part of every day trying to think of more people she could share it with."

When Bonnie passed away in 2011, Jeff ordered one

hundred copies of *The Breakthrough* to give to the people who attended her funeral. And in his remarks at the service, Jeff shared about the last copy that Bonnie had given away before she died. It was to a man named Gene, whom Bonnie had worked with for many years. He had heard of her illness and had come to visit her just a few days before she passed away. When Jeff saw Gene several days later, he asked him if he had read the book yet. Gene said that not only had he read the book, he had also called the church to sign up for an Alpha course.

Through a variety of media and material, you can take the pressure off of your own words, even as you feed and water the tender shoots of faith that are developing in your friends.

WATCH FOR "PEOPLE ON THE VERGE" WHO CROSS OUR PATHS

When the apostle Paul writes in 1 Corinthians 3:6, "I planted the seed, Apollos watered it, but God has been making it grow," he identifies a natural process by which many people come to faith in Jesus. Sometimes it's through encounters with several Christians, and we may have just a small part in helping them along their journey. Still, we should always be ready, "in season and out of season," to present the gospel or to "give the reason for the hope" we have.[4]

Jesus gave us many examples of how to communicate with people we meet along the way—such as the woman at the well, Matthew at his tax collector's booth, and Zacchaeus up in a tree.[5] And we can learn some important principles from how he communicated with people:

- He cared about people and treated them with compassion.[6]

- He gave them his full attention and wasn't distracted by other people.[7]

- He asked questions.[8]

- He found a point of connection with them.[9]

- He was bold and shared what he heard from his Father.[10]

During our dash through life, we will cross the paths of many people with whom we can build relationships over months or even years. These may include an auto mechanic, hairdresser, or a person we see on the train every morning. Others will be people we meet just one time. I've had numerous conversations with taxi drivers and people I sit next to on a plane. I usually ask the Lord to give me opportunities to meet "people of peace" on my travels, and I've had some fantastic conversations as a result. Sometimes I realize that I'm simply a link in the process of nudging a person toward faith in Christ, and other times I've run across "people on the verge" and have had the privilege of praying with them to receive Christ as their Savior and Lord. Either way, it's great fun!

Using friendly, nonthreatening questions, I ask people to share about themselves. I might ask about their work, their family, or where they're from. I might also chat them up about their favorite soccer team!

At the appropriate point in our conversation, I will ask them if they believe in God. (This might happen after discussing God's blessing on them for their family.) Asking about God naturally leads to talking about heaven and hell, and I will ask whether they know if they're going to heaven. Most people will say they are, based on their doing more good things than bad things in life. I may follow up with a few more questions, such as, "On what basis are you deciding whether you've met the standard to get into heaven?" or, "What if the standard is a lot higher than what you've determined?" This is all done in a very gentle and sensitive way. I don't push on if the person isn't amenable. But often by this stage in our chat, he or she will ask me what I think. This, of course, is a great opportunity to share the wonderful news of Jesus Christ—that by repentance and faith in Jesus, he or she can be certain of going to heaven.

A number of people I've met on my travels have prayed to receive Jesus right then and there (while keeping their eyes on the road, or when we stop, if it's a taxi driver!). Some have clearly been touched by God, but they are not ready to turn their lives over to him, and others have said they will look into attending a local Alpha course. No one has ever expressed any regret or anger about our conversation.

Another question I'll often ask is this: "I believe in the

power of prayer. Is there anything I can pray about for you?" If they want prayer (and most people do) and if it's appropriate, I will pray immediately, wherever we happen to be, in the taxi or on the plane. Some people have wept while I prayed, including a taxi driver in London, and everyone has expressed gratitude for the prayer.

I've been surprised that many of the folks I've met are Christians who have strayed from God. This includes an ex-soldier I met recently in Utah. He was fresh from a tour of duty in Iraq, and although his faith had waned, he told me that his mum was a strong Christ follower. I challenged him to "suit up and get back in the saddle." He seemed to be encouraged, and the next thing I knew, he had called his mum in Florida and was handing the phone over to me! I linked her to the Alpha website (www.alphausa.org) to find a local course, and I told her I would pray for her son.

Especially with backsliding or struggling Christians, I tell them I believe that God had arranged our meeting that day, because he loves them and is reaching out to them. My goal is to always make the conversation gentle, respectful, and sensitive. This allows more people to experience God's love and his Kingdom—and some have responded by coming to faith in Christ. But even if someone is unwilling to talk about God, I still make it a point to pray silently for that person and to trust that God sees and knows the person's situation and has a plan for reaching him or her with the love of Christ.

KEEP YOUR EYES AND EARS OPEN TO THE PROMPTING OF THE HOLY SPIRIT

One area in which I desire further growth is in being more responsive to the prompting of the Holy Spirit. For various reasons, I often miss the opportunities the Lord gives to me. However, a few years ago on a flight home to Chicago, I sensed that God had a very specific question he wanted me to ask one of the flight attendants: *What miracle are you asking God for in your life?* I didn't know which flight attendant this was for, but I really wanted to be obedient to the Holy Spirit.

As our flight passed the halfway point, I put up a desperate prayer: *Lord, please lead me to the right person and give me the courage to ask the question.*

Shortly after my prayer for help, I went to the restroom, and as I came out, I saw one of the flight attendants reading a book in one of the back rows. Christmas was coming up, and I asked her whether she would have much time off for the holiday. We got into a conversation, and I felt it was right to ask the question that God had put on my heart. "So," I said, "what miracle are you asking God for in your life this Christmas?"

There was a long pause, and I noticed that tears were welling up in her eyes and falling down her cheeks. She explained that she was indeed asking for a miracle because her marriage was breaking up, and she desperately wanted God to save it. Later in the flight, she came to where I was seated and showed me a line she had just read in her book: "What miracle are you asking God for in your life?"

I've never seen that flight attendant again, and I can only hope and pray that her marriage was restored. In any event, something of the Kingdom of God broke through on that flight to Chicago, and that young woman received confirmation that God had heard her prayer and was concerned about her broken heart. God enabled me to participate in his wonderful work of spreading his love and his Kingdom on earth. My faith grew, I think the flight attendant's faith grew, and many people with whom I've shared this story have also been encouraged.

You never know who God will bring into your path and what he may ask you to do or say. However, he wants you to have a hungry heart and open eyes and ears that are sensitive to the people around you and to the prompting of the Holy Spirit within you.

BE PREPARED WITH A SIMPLE GOSPEL MESSAGE

Sharing the gospel shouldn't be complicated, and I encourage you to have an outline that you feel comfortable with and that a child could understand. There are all kinds of approaches to sharing the gospel, but if I had a few minutes to sit down with someone, here's what I would say.

First, I'd explain that there is a God. I believe that the beauty, detail, and power of creation provide compelling evidence of this. What we see around us in the natural world doesn't happen by accident. There is design in life, and we have an intuitive sense that there must be something more.

Next, I'd want to show that God himself is revealed in

the person of Jesus Christ. The historic eyewitness evidence of Jesus' teachings, miracles, death, and resurrection points to the fact that Jesus really was who he said he was—God in the flesh.

Then I'd want to share how God has personally affected *my* life. How God brought me through tragedy. How he brought healing to my marriage. How he strengthens and changes me every single day. By the way, even if you say nothing else, your own personal story of meeting and walking with Jesus Christ is incredibly powerful. Always be ready to share this as the opportunities arise.

After sharing my own story about what God has done for me personally, I would explain that he created us all to be in relationship with him, but the relationship is broken because we've put ourselves in first place, instead of God. I'd ask the person to think about how all the fighting, greed, corruption, hunger, lying, and hate in the world are caused by individuals wanting to be first and to have their own way. Scripture calls this *sin*, and it says, "All have sinned and fall short of the glory of God."[11]

It's important to explain that there must be punishment for sin, because God is just. Think about someone doing a terrible crime. There would be no doubt in your mind that there should be punishment and a consequence, in order for things to be fair. The Good News is that Jesus himself took the punishment that you and I deserve for our sin, and because of Jesus' sacrifice on the cross, we can receive God's forgiveness for our sins and his gift of eternal life! This is fantastic news, and as Scripture says, "Yet to all who did receive him, to those who believed in his name, he gave the right to become children of God."[12]

The gospel is not complicated. It's the purity of the message that makes it beautiful to those who hear it. Be quick to tell people that you still don't have all the answers, but that you've heard and experienced enough of God's love and his Scripture to put your faith in Jesus Christ. Encourage people to ask lots of questions and to continue on their search for truth. In particular, encourage them to attend Alpha.[13]

In 1 Corinthians 15:3-4, we find Paul's account of the gospel in a nutshell: "Christ died for our sins . . . he was buried . . . he was raised on the third day." If you're worried that you don't know enough theology to share your faith, remember this verse. For two thousand years, this simple message has been changing lives, and it's still effective to transform people's lives today.

BE PREPARED TO LEAD SOMEONE IN A SIMPLE PRAYER TO RECEIVE CHRIST

As you look to share your faith with your family, friends, and acquaintances, there may come a time for you to invite them to receive Jesus as their Savior and Lord. I encourage you to be prepared but not to jump the gun with this. And always be certain not to put any pressure on someone to surrender to Christ. Remember, it's ultimately the work of the Holy Spirit to convict people of their sin and to bring them to Christ.

You may feel a little bit awkward or uncomfortable when

you invite someone to surrender to Christ, but remember the power of asking questions, which can serve to alleviate pressure. You might say something like this: "After all you've experienced and heard about Jesus and his Kingdom, can you think of any reason for not trusting and committing your life to him?" If the person is really ready, here is a simple prayer he or she can say:

> God, I am so sorry for my selfish lifestyle and for the many things I have done that have hurt you and other people.
>
> Thank you, Jesus, for dying on the cross for me and for taking the punishment I deserve for my sin. Thank you for forgiving me and setting me free, and for giving me eternal life.
>
> Please come into my life and fill me with your Holy Spirit. Take first place in my heart, and give me the strength to follow you for the rest of my life. I want to live to please you.
>
> Thank you, Lord Jesus. Amen.

There are many versions of this prayer—the precise words are not important. But the following elements should always be present: *confession* (of our sin and sinfulness), *repentance* (a commitment to turn from going our own way to going God's way), *gratitude* (for Christ's sacrifice on the cross), and *supplication* (asking to be filled by the Holy Spirit).

If the person is not yet ready to come to faith in Christ,

that's fine. It's much better to wait until they are ready than to say a prayer without meaning it.

INVITE PEOPLE TO AN ALPHA COURSE

If your family members, friends, or acquaintances are not ready to make a decision, but they want to know more about Jesus and his teaching, invite them to an Alpha introductory dinner, a church event, or a Bible study. Because I have the privilege of leading Alpha's ministry in the United States, I know that introductory dinners are a safe event for people to take another step toward coming to faith in Christ. There's a free meal, lots of fun and laughter, an interesting talk, and some great stories from people who have experienced God's love while learning about Jesus.[14]

INVITE YOUR FRIENDS TO JOIN YOU AT CHURCH

I recently read about a survey undertaken by one hundred or so Christ followers who wanted to understand the times and the culture of different generations. In particular, they wanted to know how to reach Gen Xers with the gospel.[15] They decided to interview a group of four people from outside the church between the ages of twenty and twenty-five.

The responses to the usual questions were in line with the polls:

"I don't think any one religion has the corner on the truth."

"Being gay is just the way God made them."

"I think you can worship God just as well, maybe better, on your own, out in nature."

And then one of the questioners went off script and asked, "Is there anything that would make you *want* to go to church?"

There was a long pause before someone else asked, "Would it make a difference, for example, if the sermons were really good and relevant to your life?"

"Not really."

"What if they had really good music?"

"No, I don't think so."

The group tried all sorts of ideas, including convenience, relevance, programs, and seminars. But the response was always the same. There was no interest in going to church.

Finally, someone said, "Would you go to church if a good friend invited you?"

Without hesitation, all four respondents said *yes*.[16]

Some surveys I've seen show that 80 percent of respondents say they would attend church if they were simply *invited*. It's our responsibility as Christ followers to make friends with people outside the church and to invite them to meet with Jesus.

That's what it's all about: *relationships*.

First, God has called you and me into relationship with him. He has filled us with his Holy Spirit and told us to *go* and make disciples of all nations. You and I are wired by God for relationships, and if we want to be effective "fishers of people," we must follow Jesus' example and be intentional about developing friendships with people who don't know God. If you and I will simply do this, I believe we will see another *awakening* across America.

When I think about the millions of people who need to hear the good news of Jesus, I am easily overwhelmed. I sometimes wonder if my efforts are making an impact for Christ's Kingdom. But the truth is, every single life matters. Every single life is treasured. Offering just one person a chance at salvation can make a difference for all of eternity!

It reminds me of the well-known story of the small boy who came upon thousands of starfish that had washed ashore during a storm and was throwing them back into the ocean one by one. Confronted by a cynical passerby who told him he was wasting his time, that his efforts didn't matter, the boy simply picked up another starfish and tossed it into the water, saying, "I bet it matters to that one."

Similarly, there are billions of people around the world who need to know Jesus. And for the one person you might reach today, it could make an eternal difference.

When it comes to sharing the gospel, there are often times when I feel as if I'm stumbling over my words. I don't know exactly what to say, when to say it, or how to say it most effectively. But I've found that God and his Holy Spirit graciously fill in the gaps.

I take solace in the story of a young girl who sat down at the piano in the lobby of an upscale hotel and began making a terrible noise on the keys: *plink . . . plonk . . . plink*.

Just as a distinguished guest was about to complain to the hotel manager, a man sat down beside the girl and began playing along, incorporating her meager efforts into a beautiful composition. The guest later discovered that the man playing along was the girl's father, Alexander Borodin, a celebrated composer of operas and symphonies.

As Christ followers, we enjoy a similar relationship with our heavenly Father. Incredibly, God doesn't dismiss our futile efforts; he sits with us and shares in the work. He takes our *plink . . . plonk . . . plinks* and makes something beautiful out of our lives.

It's possible you're worried about your performance as a fisher of men. Maybe you wonder whether people will be annoyed by your attempts to share the Good News or you're afraid that your words will fall flat. Fortunately, we have the Great Maestro—our God—to help us. He promises to take our clumsy attempts and turn them into something grand.

God isn't asking for your *ability*. He simply wants your *availability*. He wants you to surrender your life to him, to be filled with his Holy Spirit on an ongoing basis, and to be empowered by him to be his ambassador and witness to the gospel of Jesus Christ.

The LORD himself goes before you and will be with you; he will never leave you nor forsake you. Do not be afraid; do not be discouraged.
DEUTERONOMY 31:8

Epilogue

ON MAY 8, 2014, as I was completing the final edits on this book, the most unbearable and unthinkable happened.

While Jeannie and I were still grieving the death of our youngest son, Alex, our eldest child—our beautiful, precious daughter, Rebecca—was lost to us in a tragic accident at the age of thirty-two.

May 8 was an unseasonably warm spring day in Chicago, with temperatures in the eighties. Rebecca went for a run along Lake Michigan. We believe she was trying to cool off from her exertion when she slipped from a rock wall and fell into the lake. Unable to climb back onto the rocks, she was overcome by the frigid water. Hypothermia set in, and she drowned.

I cannot describe to you the excruciating pain of losing a child. As I write this, our family is in unspeakable anguish. Why would God allow us to lose Rebecca just a few years after we lost Alex? Jeannie and I would not be human if we didn't ask that question, even though we know we will not receive answers this side of heaven.

Yet this is the great hope we have in Christ Jesus: *This is not the end.*

I keep encouraging Jeannie to "look ahead" as we weep and mourn and try to understand. Rebecca is with Jesus. Alex is with Jesus. We are looking ahead to the day when we will all be reunited, in a heaven with no grief or suffering or pain or parting. Our God left that perfect heaven to come down to earth and walk with us, on a rescue mission to bring us home. He is a suffering God: He knows about pain and brokenness. He is here with us in ours.

The mission of helping others come to know God has never felt more urgent to me than it does right now. Jesus said, "I tell you the truth, anyone who believes has eternal life" (John 6:47, NLT). I thank God that Rebecca believed. She dedicated her entire life to helping others encounter Jesus through her work as national director of youth at Alpha USA. Though Rebecca was in agony herself from the loss of Alex, she had a heart like none I've ever known for people who were struggling. She left a legacy of love to those she helped, including Jeannie and me, who had the privilege of being her mum and dad and working alongside her as she flourished in ministry.

Rebecca lived for the love of Jesus and to share it with others. A champion runner, she ran an amazing race for her heavenly Father.

*   *   *

There is one thing more I want to say, and I pray that I say it with gentleness. We have learned from the detective investigating the tragedy that there were people watching from the shore that day as Rebecca drowned. They saw her waving her arms in distress, and they heard her cries for help. They called 911 . . . but they stayed on dry land. No one went in to rescue her.

Jeannie and I harbor no bitterness or bad feelings toward them. Who is to know whether any of us would have done the same? These individuals are no doubt experiencing tremendous remorse; the last thing I want is to add to their pain.

Yet I cannot help but see a parallel between what happened to Rebecca and what is happening with us in the church today. There are people all around us who are spiritually sinking. Yes, we must pray; but it's also up to us who believe in Christ, who are called to be his hands and feet, to reach out to help them. To share the good news about Jesus. To encourage them to grasp his hand before it's too late.

As a father, I know how it feels to want all your children safely at home with you. It's the same with our heavenly Father.

*   *   *

When Rebecca awoke each morning and came downstairs to join her mother and me for breakfast, she would give us a hug and say, "It's a new day."

Brothers and sisters, today is a new day.
Let us arise and awaken to God together.

*He has made everything beautiful in its time. He has
also set eternity in the human heart; yet no one can
fathom what God has done from beginning to end.*

ECCLESIASTES 3:11

Notes

INTRODUCTION
1. John 1:46. See also Psalm 66:5.
2. Mark 16:15, NKJV; Matthew 4:19, NKJV
3. Revelation 3:2, italics added.

CHAPTER 1: AWAKENING TO GOD'S LOVE AND PURPOSE
1. I was the England and Wales Universities 800m champion in 1979, came in third in the South of England championship in 1978, and won several county/state championships and gold medals as a member of my college 4x400m team.
2. Mark 8:36, KJV
3. Romans 5:5
4. Luke 22:42; John 4:34; 5:30; 6:38; 8:29
5. Matthew 6:19-21
6. Galatians 2:20
7. John 14:21, 23; 17:4
8. 2 Corinthians 12:9
9. 1 Samuel 30:6
10. Psalm 119:105

CHAPTER 2: AWAKENING TO THE HOLY SPIRIT: POWER FOR LIVING
1. Acts 1:4-5
2. John 16:7
3. John 16:13; 1 Corinthians 12:3
4. John 6:63

5. Billy Graham, *The Holy Spirit* (Dallas: Word, 1988), 132.
6. In 2 Corinthians 13:14, "the fellowship of the Holy Spirit" refers to an intimate relationship.
7. John 14:16-17, 26; 16:13-15
8. Acts 7:51; Ephesians 4:30; 1 Thessalonians 5:19
9. Acts 18:24-26; 19:1-7
10. Luke 11:9-13
11. Romans 5:5
12. 2 Corinthians 5:14-15
13. Acts 1:8, ESV
14. Acts 2:4; 4:8, 31
15. In Ephesians 5:18, when Paul writes that we should "be filled with the Spirit," the term in the original Greek means "be being filled" with the Holy Spirit or "be ever filled and stimulated" by the Holy Spirit.
16. 2 Corinthians 11:3-4
17. Revelation 2:4, NKJV
18. Ephesians 4:29-30
19. 1 Thessalonians 5:19
20. Acts 7:51
21. 2 Corinthians 13:14; Philippians 2:1; Proverbs 4:23
22. 1 Timothy 6:12, author's paraphrase.
23. 2 Timothy 4:7
24. Jude 1:20-21
25. Graham, *Holy Spirit*, 150.
26. Galatians 5:22-23; 1 Corinthians 12:4-11
27. Mark 13:11
28. John 16:8
29. 2 Corinthians 5:14-15
30. Galatians 5:22-23
31. Hebrews 4:16; 2 Corinthians 12:9
32. Luke 11:9-13
33. John 6:29
34. 1 Corinthians 12:1-11; 14:1
35. Read and reflect on Luke 11:9-13.
36. Romans 12:1-2
37. John 16:33; Acts 14:22; 2 Timothy 3:12
38. Psalm 34:19; Hebrews 13:5-6
39. 2 Corinthians 2:14
40. John 10:10
41. Luke 1:53

CHAPTER 3: AWAKENING TO OUR CALLING: GO AND MAKE DISCIPLES

1. John 3:16
2. Luke 19:10
3. John 20:21
4. Matthew 28:19, italics added.
5. Ephesians 2:8
6. Acts 20:24
7. Ephesians 3:10-11
8. John 14:21
9. John 17:4
10. 1 Corinthians 2:16
11. Matthew 22:37-40, author's paraphrase; Matthew 28:19-20
12. C. S. Lewis, *The Problem of Pain* (New York: Macmillan, 1944), 106.
13. Ephesians 2:10
14. Matthew 6:33
15. Mark 16:15
16. Acts 4:13, NLT
17. Luke 9:3; 10:4; 22:35
18. Galatians 2:20
19. 2 Corinthians 3:18, NLT
20. John 12:24; Galatians 2:20
21. John 15:7-8, ESV
22. Acts 4:22
23. Acts 3:11-12
24. Acts 4:12
25. Acts 4:13
26. Acts 4:18, author's paraphrase.
27. Acts 4:20, author's paraphrase.
28. 1 John 1:1-3, NLT
29. "About Nick: His Story," Attitude Is Altitude website; www.attitudeisaltitude.com/about-nick-his-story.
30. Colossians 3:1-2
31. Ephesians 2:10
32. John 17:4
33. Ephesians 6:12
34. Galatians 6:8; 2 Peter 1:4; James 4:1-2
35. Luke 4:18
36. John 10:10
37. Luke 10:17

38. Luke 10:18
39. Ephesians 3:10-11, NLT
40. John 8:12
41. Matthew 5:14-16, MSG
42. 2 Corinthians 4:6
43. Matthew 5:14
44. 2 Corinthians 2:14, ESV
45. 1 John 5:4

CHAPTER 4: AWAKENING TO BROKENNESS

1. Psalm 40:2, NKJV
2. 1 Peter 4:1-2
3. Psalm 119:67, 71
4. Ephesians 2:10
5. Ecclesiastes 3:11
6. Isaiah 25:4
7. Jeremiah 15:16
8. 1 Kings 19:12, NKJV
9. Hebrews 4:16, NKJV
10. Isaiah 40:31, NKJV
11. Psalm 31:20, NKJV
12. Philippians 1:29
13. Psalm 119:71
14. Psalm 73:21-28; 2 Corinthians 9:8
15. Job 1:12; Luke 22:31
16. Matthew 19:29; Mark 10:29-30; Luke 18:29-30
17. 2 Corinthians 4:17-18
18. 1 Peter 1:3-4
19. Scripture teaches that God never causes evil, but he does permit evil for his eternal purposes.
20. Hebrews 12:1
21. Hebrews 4:16
22. 2 Corinthians 2:14
23. Philippians 2:12-18
24. George Müller, "Soul Nourishment First" (1841); www.tms.edu/semwivesweb/media/The%20Discipline%20of%20Prayer.pdf.
25. Nehemiah 8:10
26. Acts 26:18; Ephesians 1:18
27. Genesis 50:20
28. 2 Kings 6:17

29. Romans 8:31
30. 1 John 4:4, NKJV
31. 2 Corinthians 2:11; 11:3; 1 Peter 5:8-9

CHAPTER 5: AWAKENING TO ETERNITY

1. Psalm 39:5; 144:4, NKJV; James 4:14, NKJV
2. Ephesians 2:10
3. 1 Peter 2:10-12
4. 1 Corinthians 3:12-14; 2 Corinthians 5:10
5. Matthew 6:19-20
6. Rewards are mentioned more than one hundred times in the New Testament, including Matthew 25:21-23; 1 Thessalonians 2:19-20; 2 Timothy 4:8; Hebrews 2:9; James 1:12; 1 Peter 5:2-4.
7. Colossians 3:1-4
8. John 4:34; 5:30; 6:38; 8:29
9. Ephesians 2:8
10. 1 Corinthians 9:24-27
11. Matthew 25:14-30; Luke 19:11-27
12. Colossians 3:1-3
13. Mark 4:19-20
14. C. S. Lewis, *Mere Christianity* (New York: Macmillan, 1960), 118–119.
15. Ibid., 119.
16. Romans 12:1-2; 2 Corinthians 3:18
17. Romans 12:2
18. Elisabeth Elliot, *Shadow of the Almighty: The Life and Testament of Jim Elliot* (New York: Harper, 1958), 15.
19. Matthew 6:10
20. "Jonathan Edwards," *Stanford Encyclopedia of Philosophy*; http://plato .stanford.edu/entries/edwards.
21. Jonathan Edwards, "The Christian Pilgrim," Sect. II, 3, in Henry Rogers, *The Works of Jonathan Edwards*, vol. 1 (London: F. Westley and A. H. Davis, 1835), 244.
22. Ibid., lxiii.
23. Matthew 6:19-21
24. At today's valuation, C. T. Studd gave away the equivalent of several million dollars in his early years of following Christ.
25. Norman P. Grubb, *C. T. Studd: Cricketer and Pioneer* (Fort Washington, PA: CLC Publications, 1933), 145.
26. Ibid., 124.

CHAPTER 6: AWAKENING TO OPPORTUNITY: A BIGGER VISION

1. John 6:28, ESV
2. John 6:29, ESV
3. Esther 4:14
4. Romans 12:2
5. Philippians 4:19, AMP
6. John 6:1-15
7. Luke 12:48
8. 2 Corinthians 5:10
9. John 12:24-25, NKJV
10. 1 Peter 1:7, NLT
11. Psalm 16:6
12. Adapted from Corrie Ten Boom with Jamie Buckingham, *Tramp for the Lord* (Fort Washington, PA: CLC Publications, 1974), 55–57.
13. 1 Corinthians 1:26-31
14. Another example of how God can bring unity throughout his church is through a coalition of leaders called Mission America. Under the banner of "Prayer, Care, Share," the coalition is currently working on the LOVE2020 initiative to reach every household across America with the love of Christ by 2020. See www.love2020.com.
15. Matthew 13:23; Mark 4:20
16. Proverbs 4:23, AMP

CHAPTER 7: AWAKENING TO GOD'S PROVISION: HOW TO BECOME FISHERS OF MEN

1. Matthew 4:19, ESV
2. John 5:30; 6:38; 8:29, author's paraphrase
3. John 5:30, NLT
4. Acts 17:28; Romans 11:36; 1 Corinthians 8:6
5. John 16:8-14; Ephesians 2:8-10
6. D. L. Moody, *Secret Power: Or the Secret of Success in Christian Life and Work* (Chicago: F. H. Revell, 1881), 37.
7. 2 Corinthians 5:20
8. John 15:4-8
9. Hebrews 13:20-21
10. Acts 16:30-34
11. Hebrews 4:16
12. Luke 18:1-8
13. James 5:16
14. Romans 8:26

15. Colossians 1:9
16. 1 Samuel 3:1-14
17. Winston Churchill, speech at Harrow School, October 29, 1941.
18. Matthew 6:10
19. Luke 10:2
20. Romans 1:20
21. Romans 2:4
22. John 1:14, MSG
23. John 17:15
24. *Forty Thousand Quotations: Prose and Poetical*, comp. Charles Noel Douglas (London: George G. Harrap, 1904), 1988.
25. James 1:27
26. I recognize that many non-Christians do not like to be referred to as *lost*. They feel it's condescending. But based on Luke 19:10, I define "the lost" as folks who have simply not yet come to faith in Jesus. They're the ones whom Jesus came to rescue. (And such were you and I at one time.) They're the ones to whom we're called to *go*.
27. I believe I first heard this statement from my friend Derek Rust.
28. See Luke 10:1. Jesus sent his disciples out two by two.
29. Ecclesiastes 4:12
30. Galatians 6:2
31. Esther 4:14
32. Matthew 6:10
33. Luke 10:2
34. 1 John 5:14-15
35. Luke 10:6
36. Luke 10:1-6
37. Groundbait fishing, which is not as common in the United States as it is in Europe and the UK, involves casting a type of bait into the water to attract fish to the fishing area. For an interesting article and background on this technique, see http://bankfisher.com/Patch/Groundbait.html.
38. Matthew 11:19; Luke 7:34
39. Blessing is at the heart of God's purpose for us: "I will bless you . . . and you will be a blessing" (Genesis 12:2).
40. Luke 10:9
41. Hebrews 13:20-21

CHAPTER 8: AWAKENING TO THE NETS: HOW TO DRAW IN THE FISH

1. 2 Corinthians 6:1-2, italics added.
2. Acts 4:12

3. 2 Corinthians 6:3
4. John 13:35
5. 1 Corinthians 13:4
6. 1 Corinthians 13:7, NLT
7. John 3:27; Acts 17:28; Romans 11:36; 1 Corinthians 8:6
8. John 16:8
9. 2 Corinthians 4:6
10. James 2:13
11. Micah 6:8
12. John 3:7-8
13. John 10:10; 2 Peter 1:3-4
14. Psalm 23:5-6; Romans 5:3-5; 2 Corinthians 4:17; 1 Peter 1:3-8; James 1:2-4
15. John 10:10, NKJV
16. Galatians 5:22-23, NLT
17. Luke 10:1
18. John 6:12
19. If you've had the death of a loved one or some other deep sorrow, there may need to be a time of healing and grieving before you're ready to help others.
20. James 1:17

CHAPTER 9: AWAKENING TO THE CATCH: HOW TO LAND THE FISH

1. Hebrews 11:3, AMP
2. For more information, see www.bibleseries.tv/youversion-bible-app-2, and http://app.jesusfilmmedia.org.
3. Gerard Long, *The Breakthrough* (Deerfield, IL: AlphaUSA, 2009).
4. 2 Timothy 4:2; 1 Peter 3:15
5. Matthew 9:9-13; Luke 19:1-10; John 4:1-30
6. Matthew 9:36; 14:14; 15:32; 20:34
7. Mark 10:46-52
8. Luke 5:23; 6:39, 41-42; 8:25
9. John 4:7-26, 39-42; 11:28-44
10. John 8:3-12
11. Romans 3:23
12. John 1:12
13. Or another course introducing them to Jesus Christ.
14. To find an Alpha course near you, go to alphausa.org and type in your zip code under "Find a Course."

15. This survey was conducted around 2004. The equivalent age group today would be Gen Y, born between the early 1980s and early 2000s.
16. Adapted from Randy Newman, *Questioning Evangelism* (Grand Rapids: Kregel, 2004), 258–259.

Acknowledgments

In this book, I've attempted to pass on the lessons and experiences I've learned on my journey. I want to express my deepest thanks to my wife, Jeannie, and my three precious children, Rebecca, Ben, and Alex. Thank you for being patient with me and for your forgiveness for my many faults and errors. Many thanks also to my parents, Derry and Bridget Long, and my siblings, Jax, Kim, and Will, for your love and kindness to me.

I owe a huge debt to the many people who made this book possible. First, I want to thank Jeannie, for her encouragement to keep going, and Rebecca, for her detailed edits. Thanks to my mum, who gave such encouragement, as well as some helpful comments. I'm grateful to our good friends George and Judy Kohl, who have journeyed with us over the last few years. Their love, encouragement, and prayers are so powerful, and greatly appreciated.

I'm very thankful for my friends at Alpha who have helped and encouraged me in writing this book. I'm grateful to the Alpha USA board members—Mark Emery (chair), Cate Jansma, Chris Sadler, and Bishop Mike Byrnes—who provided helpful comments. Also, I thank Sandy Millar for his comments, and most of all, for his encouragement.

I want to thank Jesse Kohl for her wonderful spirit and encouragement, and for patiently editing many versions of the manuscript. I'm grateful to Erik Wolgemuth for his encouragement, support, and belief in this project, and for his helpful comments and edits.

I want to thank all my friends at Tyndale Momentum as we partner together to encourage Christ followers to be more intentional in reaching those outside the church. I thank Jan Long Harris for catching the vision and supporting this project. My editor, Dave Lindstedt, thank you for your very helpful adjustments to the structure and content of the book. I thank the copy editors, Brittany Buczynski, Sarah Kelley, and Leah Kelley, for their diligence and skill. Also, many thanks to Sharon Leavitt for her support and encouragement, and to the sales and marketing teams led by Dave Endrody and Yolanda Sidney.

Also, I thank my friends and colleagues at Alpha USA, who have supported and encouraged this initiative. In particular, many thanks to Andrey Tsupruk, who did a great job of managing the marketing and sales of the book and in coordinating activities with the various teams.

I also want to thank Nicky and Pippa Gumbel for developing Alpha to be such a fantastic "on-ramp" for people to meet

Jesus Christ; and Tricia Neill, who has worked tirelessly to help roll out Alpha around the world.

Finally and most of all, I'm overflowing with thanks and praise to Jesus Christ. It's only through his grace that we even exist. To also participate with him in this incredible rescue mission is truly incredible.

About the Author

Gerard Long is a minister, evangelist, author, motivational speaker, and former banking executive. He is currently the executive director of Alpha USA, a nonprofit organization that introduces people to Christianity through courses supported by multidenominational churches in more than 169 countries. More than three million people have taken an Alpha course in the United States and more than twenty-four million worldwide.

ALL AUTHOR PROCEEDS FROM THIS
BOOK WILL BE DONATED TO THE
MINISTRY OF ALPHA USA.

Where are my keys
Am I at the right job
Is there more to life than this
Alpha
Everyone has questions
Alpha is a series of interactive sessions that freely explore the basics of the Christian faith in a friendly, honest and informal environment. No pressure. No follow up. No charge.
Start an Alpha near you. alphausa.org #RunAlpha